Leading Yourself

FIND MORE JOY, MEANING,
AND OPPORTUNITIES
IN THE JOB YOU
ALREADY
HAVE

Leading

Yourself

(DESPITE
IMPERFECT BOSSES,
WEIRD ECONOMIES,
LETHARGIC COWORKERS,
ANNOYING SYSTEMS,
AND TOO MANY DELIVERABLES)

ELIZABETH LOTARDO

WILEY

Published by John Wiley & Sons, Inc., Hoboken, New Jersey.
Published simultaneously in Canada.

For general information on our other products and services or for technical support, please contact our Customer Care Department within the United States at (800) 762-2974, outside the United States at (317) 572-3993 or fax (317) 572-4002.

Wiley also publishes its books in a variety of electronic formats. Some content that appears in print may not be available in electronic formats. For more information about Wiley products, visit our website at www.wiley.com.

Library of Congress Cataloging-in-Publication Data:

Names: Lotardo, Elizabeth, author. | John Wiley & Sons, publisher.
Title: Leading yourself : find more joy, meaning, and opportunities in the
   job you already have / Elizabeth Lotardo.
Description: Hoboken, New Jersey : Wiley, [2024] | Includes index.
Identifiers: LCCN 2024014708 (print) | LCCN 2024014709 (ebook) | ISBN
   9781394238705 (hardback) | ISBN 9781394238729 (adobe pdf) | ISBN
   9781394238712 (epub)
Subjects: LCSH: Career development. | Success in business.
Classification: LCC HF5381 .L666 2024 (print) | LCC HF5381 (ebook) | DDC
   650.1—dc23/eng/20240506
LC record available at https://lccn.loc.gov/2024014708
LC ebook record available at https://lccn.loc.gov/2024014709

Cover Design: Paul McCarthy

SKY10077588_061824

To my son . . . you are never powerless.

Contents

Contents

Introduction

"I don't like to gamble, but if there's one thing I'm willing to bet on, it's myself."

—Beyoncé

I was never more optimistic and excited about the working world than I was before I entered it.

The month before I graduated from college, I was hanging out in a bar with a group of friends. We were sharing updates about what we'd be doing after graduation.

During school, I had waitressed, tutored, and nannied, but now, I was about to set out on my first full-time professional gig. I gushed to my friends about the amazing job I had gotten as an Account Manager at an ad agency.

Most of my friends were equally enthused to be embarking on their "grown-up" careers. One was starting work as a teacher, and another was an entry-level engineer. Two had jobs selling software, one was going into consulting. Our eyes were wide and we felt ready to take on the exciting opportunities ahead. We were finally *adults* (or at least, that's what we thought).

Flash-forward 10 months later; we got together again, at the same bar, even sitting in the same corner booth. Yet, the energy was drastically different. Most of us felt jaded, some even defeated. Only a few in the group were holding on to the enthusiasm we all had less than a year ago.

It was discouraging, to say the least. Perhaps you've experienced similar disillusionment yourself.

You apply for what seems like a great job, you eagerly prep for the interview, and you make sure all your references are in order. You ooze enthusiasm during the interview process. When you first get the offer, you're elated. You call your partner, your parents, or your friends, gushing about how excited you are to take this next step.

Then somehow, a year or so later, your dream job becomes the very job you're dreading on Monday morning. The projects you were excited about don't feel as inspiring anymore. The changes you wanted to make seem laborious instead of empowering. And the coworkers who once seemed so awesome are now a little bit annoying.

You may have assumed that I was one of the few 20-somethings at the bar that night who still felt a zest for careerhood. Sadly, I wasn't. Less than seven months into the job I was once thrilled to get, I felt totally empty.

Yet, this all-too-common career comedown didn't happen to *all* of us sitting there in the booth. Just most of us. Three members of the group were still just as excited as they had been before we started our jobs. The rest of us assumed those three got lucky. They probably had better offices, better bosses, or more opportunities at work.

Spoiler: They didn't get lucky. In fact, one still-ambitious, optimistic changemaker had the exact same job at the same company as another friend who was currently miserable.

In hindsight, I now see that those three people were leading themselves. They had shifted, from waiting to creating, from reactive to proactive, and from powerless to powerful, all within the constraints of a normal corporate job.

While the majority of us were hoping meaning, joy, and opportunities would come out of our work experiences, they were willing it into existence.

At the time, I didn't know what they were doing differently. All I knew was that they seemed happier and more fulfilled than I was. It's funny how a single event sticks with you, and as time marches on, you find yourself unpacking it more deeply.

As I moved through my career, working with different organizations, I started noticing how crazy it is that people with the exact same job (and sometimes even the same boss) experience wildly different realities at work. Time and time again, I watched one person flourish in their job, while their counterpart in the same role was floundering.

In retrospect, that scene at the bar makes total sense. I was right, those three people were experiencing more meaning, joy, and opportunities than the rest of us. What I was wrong about was assuming that they got lucky.

Since that time, I've deepened my studies. I've unpacked why some people can thrive in imperfect conditions. Not just survive enough to not get fired, but actually experience fulfillment through the messiness. While others, in the same circumstances, feel uninspired, disengaged, and often, powerless.

Ten years after spotting the power of self-leadership in that bar, and seven years after coining the phrase "leading yourself" on LinkedIn Learning, I now see clearly that leading yourself is the difference between being happy and successful at work versus being bored and miserable.

Leading yourself is both a philosophy and a skillset that many of us bar-goers did learn, after several years of painstaking progress (at least in my case).

For some people, like my three special friends, leading yourself is innate. For most people, me included, it's not.

Over time, we all got better at self-leadership, the thing that came so naturally to those special three. We adjusted our expectations of prefect, learned to control the controllable, and got really clear about what we wanted work to be.

No matter where you are, things probably aren't perfect right now. Maybe parts of your job suck, or your boss doesn't listen, or your industry is a little behind. Maybe this isn't your dream job, your coworkers aren't your best friends, and you don't see a clear path to anything beyond Friday. Maybe things are actually pretty good, but you can't shake the gnawing feeling that they could be better. This book is going to meet you where you are.

Instead of waiting for the perfect job, the perfect boss, or the perfect market conditions, you take the reins now. You can create the work experience you want in the job you already have.

Why I Wrote This Book

In my last decade of consulting, I've read a ton of business books. The vast majority of them fail to make any lasting impact for two reasons:

- *They're aimed at the C-Suite* . . . of which 99% of people are not in. Most people have zero direct reports. They don't control the products their organizations sell, the systems they use, or the goals they set. That's not a bad thing, it just means pie-in-the-sky projections about the future of business are generally unhelpful, especially if you're an individual contributor.

- *They're frighteningly abstract* . . . Business books are full of studies and theories that show the benefits of innovation, purpose, and kindness in the workplace. These are things we instinctively already know. Obviously, people have more ideas when they're not being bullied at work, and when someone cares about something, they try harder. You don't need a book to tell you that. What's generally lacking is what do you **DO** with that information, at your actual job.

This is a book about real-life work, not theoretical musings from an executive think tank.

My goal is to give you the tools to help you navigate all the imperfections of the working world in a way that leaves you happier and more successful. This book is full of talk tracks, templates, and examples from people at normal jobs inside of normal companies.

We're going to cover things like:

- What do you say to your micromanager on Monday morning? (Chapter 8)

- What do you do when all the people on the project you're leading stop responding to your emails? (Chapter 11)

- How do you keep yourself from going insane through another re-org? (Chapter 3)

Here's the tough truth: If you're frustrated with your organization, your job, your coworkers, or your boss, you're the one paying the price. Not them. You're the one who's not going to do your best work, you're the one who is going to wake up in a bad mood, and you're the one whose career will suffer.

- What do you do if your boss or organization sets unrealistic goals? (Chapter 5)
- How do you prioritize when everything feels urgent? (Chapter 6)
- How can you not be mad every day when you disagree with the direction your organization is taking? (Chapter 9)

Leading yourself is about controlling the controllable. It's owning, from whatever seat you're in, your work experience. Your mindset, how you show up, and the relationships you build are what you control. Nothing else. That truth can be defeating or empowering, depending on how you look at it.

The world of work is annoying sometimes, no matter where you work or who you work for, and it's up to you to navigate that in a way you're proud of.

Leading yourself can help you do that.

Defining Your End Game

Think about someone you know who loves their job. They're always talking with excitement about the projects they have coming up. They have a good relationship with their boss. They're optimistic about the future, instead of afraid of it.

These people often aren't in the C-Suite. They don't work for the exclusively cool-kid companies. They don't typically have prestigious educations, unlimited resources, or generational wealth. They have ordinary jobs, at ordinary companies.

Yet, their work experience is anything but ordinary. They find meaning at work, despite annoyances. They're joyful, despite bureaucracies, setbacks, and dear god, another "pivot."

You might find them admirable. You also might find them annoying. For most of us, it's a little bit of both.

The people who love their job have created a work experience worth loving, and you can do the same. Maybe not today, but you can set the wheels in motion.

Let me be clear on what I mean when I say "the work experience you want." You might not want to be the CEO. You might not even want to be a boss at all. The "ideal work experience" varies widely because people and their priorities vary widely.

Here are some examples of what the work experience **you** want could look like:

- You get promoted within 12 months to a managerial role. After that, you climb the ladder even more, making your way to executive leadership before you're 40.

- You stay in your current job. Over the coming year, the people on your team regard you as one of the best, most supportive colleagues they've ever worked with. Your network of goodwill is second to none.

- You gain autonomy to invest your brain space in things that are most interesting to you. After seeing how dialed in and strategic you are, your boss develops incredible trust in you and mostly leaves you alone.

- You make your job even more efficient and impactful, enabling you to work a four-day workweek, turn your email off at 3 p.m., or take a month's hiatus each summer to be with your family.

- Your expertise becomes so valuable that you're put in charge of the next cool innovation project. Eventually, you get an interview at a cool startup you've been stalking on LinkedIn.

Only you can define what you're after, and that will likely change over time. The mindsets, skills, and beliefs of leading yourself can help you bounce between potentially all of the above throughout your career.

Before we dive in, I'm going to be really candid. Privilege makes leading yourself a lot easier. Money, time, emotional support, physical health, a strong network . . . it helps. A lot. Not having to deal with microaggressions, biases, or downright prejudice is an intellectual and emotional freedom only a portion of the workforce experiences today.

I'm going to challenge us to run a dual path:

- We're all responsible for creating a more diverse, equitable, and inclusive world of work. Each of us has a personal duty to leave our colleagues, our customers, and our organizations better than we found them.

- At the same time, we're going to work with what we've got. That is not synonymous with tolerating injustice. It's acknowledging the very real inequities, while at the same time, charting our own way and creating the unique future we desire.

What We Want Out of Work

How often do you experience the feeling of joy at work? Is it after a good performance review, a lunch with your colleagues, or finally achieving inbox zero?

In a recent *Harvard Business Review* survey, nearly 90% of respondents said that they expect to experience a substantial degree of joy at work, yet only 37% report that such is their actual experience.[1] Even for those who are experiencing a substantial degree of joy at work, there's always room for more.

Joy is connected to meaning; those who view their role as critical to the success of the team are much more likely to experience joy at work. Those who feel their talents are utilized effectively are even more so.

That's not surprising. When we feel like we're making a difference, we're more likely to feel joyful. Finding delight in something you view as a perfunctory waste of time is nearly impossible.

Joy and meaning are what we want *today*, but as humans, we often find our minds concocting the next play. The retention research bears that out. Seventy-six percent of employees are looking for opportunities to expand their careers. Eighty-six percent of employees say they'd switch jobs for one with more chances to grow.[2]

Most disgruntled work experience stems from a lack of (at least) one of these three crucial elements: Joy, meaning, or opportunities.

The mistake I, and so many of my peers, made, is assuming that you can't make those things yourself. Is it easier if all of that is present the moment you onboard? Yes, but the absence doesn't have to be permanent.

No career will be an end-to-end experience of joy, meaning, and opportunities. If it was, you would pay your boss and we'd call it Disneyland. Yet, with you in the driver's seat, joy, meaning, and opportunities can be more frequent.

What We Hate About Work

We watch shows about how dreary *the office* can be. The comic strip *Dilbert* ran in thousands of newspapers for 30 years. There was even a movie about three friends who conspired to murder their awful bosses. In humor, there's truth. Yes, work can be fulfilling, rewarding, highly profitable, and a worthy endeavor. It can also be really frustrating.

In all the interviews I've done for this book, the research I've pored over, and in my own experiences, there are clear themes. No matter the industry, no matter the size of the organization, and no matter how well-intended everyone is, the inevitable woes arise.

Here are some of the most common grievances, in no particular order:

- **Imperfect bosses.** We've all heard the expression: people don't leave their jobs, they leave their managers. While it's typically more complicated than that, the expression highlights just how crucial a manager is in the satisfaction and performance of their teams. Even a great boss has their imperfect moments. In a survey of 3000 employees about what employees dislike most in a manager, incompetence, a lack of availability, and micromanagement were at the top of the list.[3]

- **Weird economics.** Are we going into a recession? Will AI spike unemployment? Why is chicken so expensive? As of writing this, according to a survey by Wolters Kluwer Blue Chip Economic Indicators, there's a 50% chance of a recession in the next 12 months[4] . . . so, there's also a 50% chance there won't be a recession in the next 12 months. Not exactly reassuring in either direction.

- **Lethargic coworkers.** According to CNBC, 90% of Americans have a coworker who annoys them and 55% of people reported that they still get annoyed with their coworkers several times a week in a remote vs. in-office environment.[5] One leader I spoke to said, "My actual job is easy, it's working with the other 748 people here that can be challenging."

- **Annoying systems.** Fill out a timesheet in military time, share your files on that platform, but not as a PDF, only a doc, your email that you read on your phone has somehow vanished on your desktop, oh, and don't EVER click the link. If you find yourself overwhelmed and frustrated by systems that claim to make work easier, you're not alone. McKinsey reports that employees spend 1.8 hours every day searching and gathering information.[6] A Compucom survey cited that the average employee faces 18 technical frustrations during the work week.[7]

- **Too many deliverables.** When technology, the economy, and competitors are changing quickly, the project roadmap changes too. And rarely are things removed – they're just piled on. In a multinational survey with more than 1,600 responses, through various industries, only 6% of people say they do *not* experience stress at work.[8] So, turns out, most of us are lying awake at night ruminating, at least some of the time.

This research isn't compiled from the "worst companies ever" list. These things (though incredibly frustrating) are *normal*. Annoyance is an inevitable part of the work experience, but what you do in the face of it is your choice. With the exact same annoyance, one person will be derailed for weeks while another rolls their eyes and moves on.

We want work to be joyful, meaningful, and a gateway to opportunities. But, our purest intentions of fulfillment are often marred by clunky systems, busy people, and the perils of uncertainty.

Yet somehow these things don't get in *everyone's* way.

You'll notice that I've left out a very popular grievance: *pay*.

Because it's not an "always-present-must-accept-at-least-a-little-bit annoyance." It's more malleable.

If you are not being paid a competitive wage, based on your skills and the value you provide to the organization, you're in a gray area. You may accept that less-than-stellar paycheck in exchange for more flexibility, better benefits, or an exceptional work environment. You may know that your salary now is only temporary, with a clear path to substantial raises in the not-distant future. You may be slightly grumbly about it, but not enough to change jobs right now for whatever reason, and that's fine, too.

If you are truly not being paid a *living* wage, that has to change first. No amount of leading yourself can override food insecurity, a lack of housing, or inadequate medical care. To employ the mindsets of a self-starter, you must be at baseline economic survival. No company is perfect, but some companies are cruel. We'll talk about more distinctions between "imperfect" and "cruel" but when it comes to compensation, not paying a living wage is cruel. If that describes your employer, you need to put every ounce of mental effort you have into finding a new job. Skip to Chapter 12.

What If . . .

You might be thinking . . . but you don't know *my* boss. You don't know how frustrating *my* company is. There's no way this could work for *me*.

Maybe you're right. There's a chance you could diligently employ the strategies in this book and nothing changes. Every shred of research would indicate otherwise, but anything could happen. You're a grown-up; you can dig your heels into the sand if you want to.

But let me ask you this: What if you started proactively leading yourself . . . and *everything* changed?

What if you woke up with more energy?

What if you had a better relationship with your boss?

What if you didn't want to roll your eyes at your inbox or count down until your next vacation?

What if you got to bring the most authentic, ambitious, and engaged version of you to work every day?

What would that feel like?

You might have to power through some awkwardness. There will likely be setbacks, frustrations and disappointments. It won't break you. Really, it's not *that* hard.

There's a saying I fall back on when I'm getting the courage to start something new.

"The best time to plant a tree was 100 years ago. The second-best time is today."

The best time to start leading yourself is when you're starting your first job at age 15. The second-best time is today.

We all deserve to feel purpose at work. We deserve to have our expertise valued, to have opportunities to grow, and to work with people we enjoy (most of the time).

You have the power to give that gift to yourself.

Part I

Mindset: Managing the Space Between Your Ears

Our mental frame is a filter through which we process our lives. At work, our mental frame impacts how we perceive our job, our boss, our customers, our company, and even our own contribution.

People who lead themselves lean on four distinct mental abilities that propel their daily actions and work experiences:

- They find purpose in the everyday.
- They train their brains to avoid mental ruts.
- They act in the face of fear.
- They can tolerate uncertainty.

As we unpack these four abilities, we'll look at why they work and how you can leverage them in your own work life. We'll also look at the very real obstacles to maintaining these abilities and how you can overcome them.

Chapter 1

Finding Purpose in a Normal Job

*"Our deepest desire is to make a difference, and our darkest fear is
that we won't."*

—Lisa Earle McLeod

A key underpinning of experiencing more joy and meaning at work is
knowing that your work makes a difference. Having a sense of higher
purpose, knowing that our work matters, is what enables us to feel fulfilled
even when things don't go perfectly.

The good news is, you don't have to quit your job and join the Peace
Corps to feel greater purpose at work.

If your work impacts your customers, your colleagues, or the commu-
nities you serve, you're making a difference. Otherwise, your job wouldn't
exist. The challenge is, for most of us, the larger impact of our work is often
buried in an overflowing inbox. Or it's passed from department to department, eventually escaping our field of vision.

We're tackling purpose as the first mindset in leading yourself because
job satisfaction and long-term motivation depend upon us knowing that
our work counts for something beyond a monetary transaction. Without
purpose, feeling engaged is an impossibility.

People who are leading themselves don't wait for the big rah-rah meeting or the corporate purpose video to feel good about their job. Instead,
they tether themselves to a personal sense of higher purpose that fuels them
through big goals and tough setbacks. Clarity about how you make a difference (in your regular job) is imperative for energy.

Your company may be changing the world, or they may be just
improving the world of accounting. No matter what they're doing, finding

purpose in your job is about directing your site line toward the impact of your personal contribution.

Unfortunately, most job descriptions aren't particularly inspiring. They're functional, like a to-do list. Rarely is it perfectly articulated why the role exists and what impact the role has beyond simply completing the aforementioned functional tasks. Waking up every day to a punch list of disconnected action items is a quick path to burnout.

The consequences of our collective lack of meaning and purpose at work became painfully obvious during COVID.

At the start of the COVID-19 pandemic, a large percentage of the workforce went home. At first, people were just happy to do their jobs and they jumped in doing what their company needed to stay afloat. But as weeks turned into months, and we began to question if we would ever leave the house again, our adrenaline faded, and we started to ponder: What am I actually doing with my days? Does it even matter?

You probably remember where you were when it started to get "real." The swanky office sat still, the boujee coffee bar empty, and the glass whiteboards bare.

The peripheries of cheerful colleagues and office perks that made work mostly tolerable faded away. All that was left was you, your laptop, and *the work*.

In a crisis, you tend to reevaluate your life. Something like a job loss, a health scare, or a death in the family stops you in your tracks. You ask yourself: Who am I? What am I doing with my life? Am I happy where I am?

Typically, these kinds of existential experiences happen (mostly) in isolation, to a singular person or family facing a challenge. At any given time only a small percentage of the population is thrown into "reflection" mode.

But in 2020, it happened on a global scale. Personal reflection occurred en masse and it fundamentally changed the way we live and the way we work. To be clear, people have always craved purpose and meaning, but historically, most of us settled for a paycheck, some perks, and a nice work environment. Not anymore.

A portion of those people are probably happier now. This pandemic-induced awakening gave many people the courage to leave abusive bosses, toxic work environments, and dead-end paths. However, for most of those people, making a massive career change didn't deliver the inspirational high that they were hoping for.

In fact, inspiration was so apparently lacking in these new opportunities that many returned back to the job they left. A 2023 *Harvard Business Review* report showed that 28% of new hires in a multi-year study were boomerang hires (employees who had resigned within the previous 36 months).[1]

> For millions of people, the way work had been done before was no longer cutting it. The Great Resignation ensued. People changed jobs or industries or completely reconstructed their lives in the quest for fulfillment.

Further research reported that 43% of people who resigned during the Great Resignation admitted they were better off at their old job and 41% felt they quit their job too quickly.[2]

Despite significant numbers of people making moves to seek more meaning and purpose at work, employee engagement remained relatively flat during this time of upheaval. According to Gallup, in 2012, 33.6% of the US workforce was actively engaged, meaning nearly 70% of people were not emotionally invested in their jobs.[3] A decade later, the numbers remain almost unchanged. In 2022, 32% of the US workforce was actively engaged (a scant 1.6% lower than 10 years earlier).[4]

So, as the saying goes, the grass isn't always greener. Despite a massive shift in the job seeker landscape, plus substantial raises and incentives, things are kind of . . . the same.

The Purpose Backstory

The quest for purpose that fueled the Great Resignation isn't a new human aspiration. Our search for meaning has been eternal. For centuries, in every part of the world, people have expressed a fundamental desire to make a difference.

The first traces of "purpose" as a concept date back to about 350 BCE. Aristotle often referenced the Greek term *eudaimonia,* a broad concept used to describe the highest good humans could strive toward – a life "well lived."[5] For many years, scholars translated eudaimonia to mean "happiness." Now we know the concept is more nuanced than that. Eudaimonia is actually closer to "contentment through virtue."

Over the span of a few centuries, the idea of "purpose" wove its way through the world, becoming the core of religions, the galvanizing force behind revolutions, and the inspiration powering breakthrough innovations.

Eventually, purpose made its way from a philosophical musing to a cornerstone of the working world. Contrary to what the purpose-washing headlines of the 2020s would lead you to believe, purpose in the *workplace* isn't a recent development.

If you've spent any time on the internet, you've likely seen the "Ikigai" graphic, a Japanese concept that emerged a few thousand miles East and a few centuries after Aristotle.

It looks so straightforward in Figure 1.1, doesn't it? What you love, what you're good at, what the world needs, and what you're paid for, magically coalesce to produce your *purpose.* Just bring a few circles together and

Figure 1.1   Ikigai representation.

your life is filled with meaning, fun, and success. But people and careers are inherently messy.

I doubt that someone's perfect confluence or Ikigai presents as "entry-level accountant" or "junior data analyst." Those titles (and the vast majority of other corporate job titles) don't have a particularly noble ring to them, even though they may be of crucial importance.

You're More Than Your Job

We tie so much emotion, achievement, and history to our corporate identity. In many interactions, what we do defines who we are. That's why we feel so empty when our job is seemingly not "aligned."

Here's an emblematic example – when you sit down on the airplane, the extrovert next to you, without fail, will ask you, "What do you do?" It's kind of a tell about our culture, that people will ask you this question before asking your name.

When you were little, teachers would ask you, "What do you want to be when you grow up?" As if you weren't already a person in your own right, the implication is that you become your profession.

What's the first question your parents ask when they learn you're seeing someone? "Where do they work?" Which as we all know is the shorthand for: what's their social status, how educated are they, and how much money do they make?

Our world has no problem reinforcing an (incorrect) belief: you are your job. Intellectually, you know that you're more than your job. However, when we spend most of our waking hours at work, and our society holds up "work" as a crucial part of our identity, it's only natural that our human desire for purpose permeates into our careers. The challenge is, we spend our energy *looking* for purpose, instead of *creating* it.

It's OK If You're Not Passionate

"Purpose" and "passion" are often used somewhat interchangeably to describe highly motivated people. However, there's a little bit of nuance that has a major impact on how we experience our jobs (and how our organizations experience us).

Let's start with definitions: Passion is when you're excited about your work. Purpose is when you believe your work is making an impact.

Ideally, you're both passionate and purposeful. You're personally elated at what you do and you know you're making a difference. But if you had to pick between purpose and passion, which would you choose? Which would have a bigger impact on your work performance?

In the book *Great at Work: The Hidden Habits of Top Performers,* Morten Hansen revealed a fascinating link between passion, purpose, and performance.[6] In a study of more than 5,000 employees and managers, here's what he found:

- People who are low on both passion and purpose are in the bottom 10% of performers. No surprises there; if you think something is boring and meaningless, you're probably not going to be an overachiever.

- Also unsurprisingly, people with both passion and purpose (those who are excited about their job and feel it has meaning) are in the 80th percentile of performers, far above average.

Here's where it gets interesting:

- The people who were passionate – who expressed excitement about their jobs – were still poor performers if they lacked purpose. They rated in the 20th percentile of Performers. Quite low.

- Compare that with the employees who did not feel passion, who thought their work was kind of boring, yet had a strong sense of purpose. They scored in the 64th percentile of performance. Pretty solid (see Figure 1.2).

That's a huge difference, and honestly, kind of a relief. If you want to feel engaged, you do not have to be passionate all of the time. There are parts of every job that are annoying, laborious, and not inspiring. Evaluating

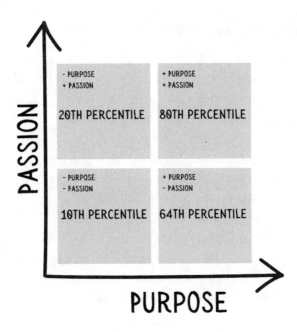

Figure 1.2 Passion versus purpose.

your job exclusively through the lens of "How excited am I every day?" is setting yourself up for disappointment.

Hopefully, you're excited at least some of the time. Being passionate is a great feeling. But that feeling can be fleeting, whereas purpose is more constant.

Passion waxes and wanes based on what's going on around you. It's easier to feel passion when something new comes your way, like being assigned an exciting new project. It's also easier to lose your passion when things go poorly, like when your proposal for something gets rejected.

Purpose is more steadfast; it's also more likely to be shared. When people are counting on you to make a difference, and you have partners in your pursuit (colleagues, customers, etc.), you're more likely to push through a setback or rally on a tough day.

If you want to feel better about your job, focus on how it makes a difference, instead of trying to convince yourself that it's the most exciting thing in the world.

Purpose and Our Health

Héctor García studies Ikigai – the Japanese philosophy with "purpose" at the core of a life well lived. He says that this sense of purpose is innate to Japanese people: "It's a natural thing – they have a strong sense of purpose. Dedication and perseverance is everywhere in Japan."[7]

Perhaps not coincidentally, Japan is ranked top five in the world for life expectancy, with women expected to live 87.97 years and men expected to live 81.91 years.[8] Of course, there are a lot of variables to a long life, but it's worth considering the impact of emotional fulfillment.

You've probably experienced situations where you felt the physiological impact of purpose. Think about a time in your life when you were proud. It doesn't have to be at work. Maybe it's when you shipped a product that worked, maybe it's when your kid finally scored a soccer goal after you practiced with them all weekend. When was a time you felt your heart about to burst with pride?

You likely remember the feeling on a physical level. You weren't tired, no matter how much (or little) you had slept. Your body felt lighter, your eyes more open, and your jaw relaxed. That moment feels like a release from the dreary daily drumbeat of to-do.

> The feeling of "purpose" serves up an incredible neurological cocktail of dopamine, serotonin, and oxytocin. Our brain *loves* it, and so do our other organs.

A 2019 JAMA Network Open study found that among a group of nearly 7000 adults over age 50, those who scored highest on a scale that measured "life purpose" were less likely to die during the four-year study period.[9]

So, is micro-dosing fulfillment the key to living forever? Not entirely, but the data suggests it might help.

Purpose Creates Performance

Having a sense of purpose at work makes you happier, more grateful, and can potentially contribute to a longer life. It also makes you more successful at your actual job.

Professor and organizational psychologist Adam Grant has devoted significant chunks of his professional career to examining what motivates workers in settings that range from call centers and mail-order pharmacies to swimming pool lifeguard squads.

Grant had a hypothesis. Instead of trying the traditional corporate ways to motivate people (fear or a dangling carrot incentive), he would show employees who was positively impacted by their work. As you read Grant's two experiments, think about your own work, and who your work ultimately impacts.

In the first experiment, he studied paid employees at a public university's call center who were asked to phone potential donors to the school. It's a tough job, full of rejection. Turnover is high, the pay isn't great, and morale is often low.

Grant and a team of researchers arranged for one group of call center workers to interact with scholarship students who were the recipients of the school's fundraising largesse. It wasn't a long meeting – just a five-minute session where the workers were able to ask the student about his or her studies.

That five minutes had a major impact. A month later, callers who had interacted with the scholarship student spent more than two times as many minutes on the phone and brought in vastly more money: a weekly average of $503.22, up from $185.94.[10]

In a follow-up study, Grant focused on lifeguards at a community recreation center. A portion of the lifeguards were asked to read a few stories about how lifeguards had averted fatalities. When the impact of their work was brought to the fore, their performance shot up 40% (measured by job dedication and helping behavior).

Another portion of the lifeguards were asked to read stories from other lifeguards about why lifeguarding was a good gig, personally. Catch a sun tan, make a good living, what's not to love? That group's performance was flat. Even when they knew lifeguarding was a good job, they didn't help any more people and they weren't any more committed.

The evidence was clear: employees who know how their work has a meaningful, positive impact on others are not just happier than those who don't; they are vastly more productive, too.

23

Finding Purpose in a Normal Job

In the preceding experiments, the participants performed better and experienced more job satisfaction when someone else framed up the sense of larger meaning of their jobs (i.e., purpose). You may not have that inspirational "someone else" at work. That shouldn't stop you from tapping into your larger impact. You may be relieved to know the emotional and performance implications are exactly the same when individuals *themselves* focus on the larger impact of their work.

This even holds true in one of the seemingly most transactional professions: sales.

It's long been assumed that sales teams are primarily driven by economic incentives. After all, they're often paid on commission. Yet Dr. Valerie Good, a professor and researcher at Michigan State University, found that the top salespeople aren't cash registers at all. Her study revealed that salespeople are more likely to work harder and be more adaptable if they're motivated by the belief that one is making a contribution to a cause greater, and more enduring, than oneself, as compared to a desire for money.[11]

When we understand how our thoughts influence our behavior, we can use that power for good. Being proactive about changing your thoughts jumpstarts a cascade that ultimately changes the results (see Figure 1.3).

Figure 1.3 Purpose cycle.

Framing your thoughts around the larger impact of your work gives you more motivation and pride, which makes it easier to put forth more effort and creativity, which then produces better results.

The inverse of this cycle is also alive and well. Just ask anyone who hates their job. You may have experienced this cycle too, in a slump (see Figure 1.4).

It's hard to recognize when you're in the slump cycle and even harder to break out of it. Nobody wakes up one day and decides they hate their job and don't care anymore. It's often death by a thousand cuts: some off-base feedback, a crappy manager, an idea shot down, your friendly coworker leaves, you have to learn a clunky new system, and then, somehow, the job you were so excited about applying for becomes the bane of your existence.

Daily annoyances can cause us to lose our tether to the actual impact of our work. Maintaining a sightline to how your work makes a difference is foundational for leading yourself. It gives you energy and purpose. It's also the catalyst you need to get where you want to go, performance-wise.

Think back to what your ideal work experience is: Autonomy? Schedule freedom? Prestige? A strong network? Unless your ideal work experience is being micromanaged and underpaid, producing good work will be an integral part of getting there.

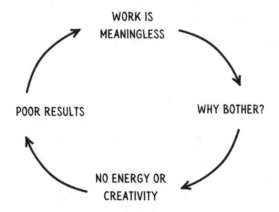

Figure 1.4 Lack of purpose cycle.

When Your Company Has a "Purpose" But You Don't Feel It

In a survey of 2,285 American professionals (across 26 industries and a range of pay levels, company sizes, and demographics) 9 out of 10 people said they were willing to earn less money to do more meaningful work.[12]

Recently, it seems like every HR and Marketing department on the planet got the "we want purpose" memo. In the 2020s, organizations were quick to tout their "purpose" in an effort to inoculate themselves against The Great Resignation, mass disengagement, or poor press.

Recruitment ads were filled with language about purpose, meaning, and nobility. *Come be part of something bigger than yourself* or *change the world with us* were tempting calls.

The challenge is, most jobs have parts that kind of just . . . suck. So, when you have to make cold calls, fill in timesheets, or show your boss how to rotate a pdf, it feels like a disruption of expectations. Aren't we supposed to be changing the world here?

Remember, despite mass changes in the employment landscape, most people were not demonstrably happier in their new job; many who left returned to their former employers and overall employee engagement remained pretty flat.

It's not that the self-proclaimed purpose-driven organizations were being untruthful. Those employees are part of something bigger than themselves. But the "how" isn't obvious, and no one is connecting the dots from functional tasks to why they matter. The more practical a role, the less obvious the connection.

Those "purpose-driven" companies have the same functional job as their less-sexily-branded counterparts.

Research by EY and Forbes Insight found that the more senior an executive is, the more confident he or she is that their organization is purpose-driven. Ninety-eight percent of CEOs surveyed agreed with the statement that "our purpose is central to our organization and is well understood by all." Yet, once you leave the C-Suite, that belief erodes, falling to 50% among vice presidents.[13]

Sound familiar?

Ideally, you have an incredibly emotionally intelligent manager and HR team with the time in their day to describe how each "to do" of your role contributes to the larger whole.

In the event you don't (most people don't), it's up to you to connect the dots. You have to draw a line from the stuff you do every day to how your company is making a difference. Again, you might not be curing diseases, healing the environment, or pouring into the next generation. Your work still matters. Your company wouldn't have customers if it didn't.

In his introduction to *Working*, writer and historian Studs Terkel positioned meaning as an equal counterpart to financial compensation in motivation. Here's what he says: "[Work] is about a search . . . for daily meaning as well as daily bread, for recognition as well as cash, for astonishment rather than torpor," he wrote.

Your CEO gives a great speech about the noble purpose of your organization at the town hall. You're inspired. Then you return to your list of deliverables, your boss is annoyed because you're behind on a project, and you failed the IT phishing test. You've only been back at your desk for 20 minutes, yet the feeling of inspiration and camaraderie is already very distant.

Among those "happy few" he met who truly enjoyed their labors, Terkel noted a common attribute: They had "a meaning to their work over and beyond the reward of the paycheck."[14]

Let's look at how you can lead yourself to become one of those "happy few."

How to Find Your Purpose (Amongst Your Deliverables)

Now that we know having a higher purpose is crucial for fulfillment at work, the burning question is how do we find our own sense of purpose amidst a pile of less-than-thrilling deliverables?

Recent PwC research revealed that the vast majority (96%) of employees believe that achieving fulfillment at work is possible. Further, employees recognize they must lead in making work more meaningful for themselves – about 80% are willing to find their own path to fulfillment.[15]

I suspect you're one of them – someone who wants to take initiative and create purpose at work, instead of waiting for someone to magically hand it to you. It's a pretty tall order, though, to independently discover a sense of fulfillment.

> Don't let the notion of "creating purpose" send you into an existential crisis. It's not as hard as it sounds and you have no deadline. So, try to relax.

Clarity about how you currently make a difference enables you to bring your sense of purpose to the fore of daily work. There are three thought-starter exercises that can help you on the road to purpose discovery. Pick the one that seems easiest to start.

Option 1: Articulate Your Ripple Effect

An impact map is an articulation of how you make a difference. It's a visual exercise to trace your impact all the way through (well beyond your inbox or performance review).

Start with writing what you do at the center of your impact map. This is your functional role, probably what you have listed on LinkedIn. How does what you do make a difference on a daily basis? Maybe you give briefs to people who need them, you crunch numbers for your organization, or you manage the messaging that gets customers to the website.

Whatever it is, write a few spokes about how you make a difference. Then ask yourself an important question. *And then what happens?* Push yourself to articulate the ripple effect.

Keep asking: and then what? And then what? Use Figure 1.5 as a guide.

For example, if you sell IT services, your impact map might look something like Figure 1.6. If your work in IT services enables your organization

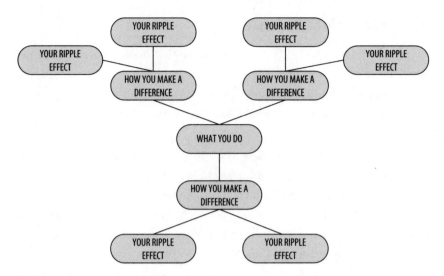

Figure 1.5 Impact map template.

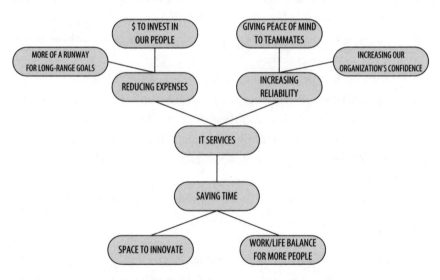

Figure 1.6 Example impact map.

to save time, what happens? People have space to innovate. Their work/life balance improves. Organization overwhelm subsides.

Once you overcome the mental awkwardness, you'll see that the things you do every day aren't seeming so small anymore.

Option 2: Explore Absence

Have you seen the movie *It's a Wonderful Life?* It's an old holiday movie that gives a lot of people (including me) the feels. The premise of the movie is that George Bailey, a banker, is visited by a guardian angel, Clarence. Clarence shows George what his life would look like without all of his good deeds and hard work.

With great clarity, George saw just how big of a difference he was making in the lives of so many people. Seeing his (imagined) absence filled him with pride. It made what he *did* do more obvious.

You can take the same mental approach, sans a guardian angel. What would happen if you didn't do your job? The skeptic in you might be wailing, "My company would find another cog to fill this meaningless hole!"

Put your inner curmudgeon aside for a moment and explore the thought train. If all your emails stopped, if the kibosh was put on all of your projects, and your deliverables never came to fruition, what would happen? Probably some grouchy coworkers. Maybe grouchy customers. Your boss would certainly not have a fun time.

Let's trace the "and then what" ripple effect. After the noticed absence, what would happen? Would your coworker be a little more bummed without you? How would that impact their day, and the way they go home to their family? Would your organization be a little less innovative? How would that play out over time? What would it mean for other people's jobs or your customers?

It's easier to see how much something matters when it suddenly stops happening.

I was working with an IT team at a major bank. We were talking about how they make a difference to their organization. One of the guys said, "No one ever notices us until something goes wrong." It's not just IT, where we gloss over the positive impact. It's everything.

Option 3: Let Other People Tell You

It's tempting to minimize our own impact. Constantly underestimating the value of your own contributions will quickly make you feel insignificant.

Oftentimes, your coworkers, boss, or customers are more acutely aware of your impact than you are yourself. I'm not suggesting you go fishing for compliments, but asking a few questions can give your brain the context it needs to feel purpose.

Here are some ideas:

- Hey! I sent that report your way last week. Did you have all the data you needed to make an informed decision?
- Just remembered we rehearsed your big presentation last week. I'm dying to know how it went!
- Did that idea we talked about land with your boss?

You probably don't want to send these questions to the CEO. Start with some friendlies to create a positive feedback loop. You can also look to customers for feedback, even if you're not customer-facing.

I was having a conversation with Jolie Miller, a Director at LinkedIn, who makes a practice of regularly engaging in LinkedIn Learning user feedback. She says, "Anyone can get in touch with what people are saying about the products their company makes. Personally, I find that to be a good touch-stone *with why I'm here*. Knowing that other people are benefiting from what we are doing in our 9-5 is grounding, and on a hard day, can help me recenter on purpose and impact. It's not all spreadsheets and numbers."

Your organization likely has some vehicle for customer feedback. Even if customers are unhappy and express needs for improvement, their feedback still shows your brain that there are actual people on the other side of this work.

When I've used these exercises in workshops, people are often stunned to see that their work has a bigger impact than they initially realized.

You needn't create a pithy purpose statement. There's no philosophical tattoo or desk plaque necessary. Purpose doesn't have to be an official "thing." It's fine if it lives as a feeling. A messy array of words, projects, and relationships, that taken together, fill you with pride.

This is the essence of leading yourself, looking around a seemingly fixed scenario (your job), and saying, *how can I find the meaning in this?*

Finding Purpose in a Normal Job

There's No Guarantee

I'm not going to guarantee you that when you find a sense of purpose you will become CEO, live forever, and also win a Nobel Peace Prize. There's some data that would suggest it's more likely, but it's an imperfect science.

What I will promise is that when you connect your work, the stuff you do on a daily basis at your normal job, to a sense of higher purpose, you'll feel a little bit better about your day. And that feeling, over time, can make a substantial difference in your life.

You might still get fired, hit by a bus, or abducted by aliens (apparently?). But you have nothing to lose by trying.

REMEMBER

- HAVING A SENSE OF PURPOSE HAS A LASTING IMPACT ON YOUR LEVEL OF EMOTIONAL FULFILLMENT, YOUR PHYSICAL HEALTH, AND YOUR PERFORMANCE AT WORK. IN THE ABSENCE OF PURPOSE, WORK MAY BEGIN TO FEEL LIKE A MEANINGLESS GRIND.

- KNOWING YOUR WORK MAKES A DIFFERENCE FUELS YOU WITH MOTIVATION AND PRIDE, WHICH ENABLES YOU TO BE MORE CREATIVE, ADAPTABLE, AND STRATEGIC IN YOUR EFFORTS. PURPOSE-DRIVEN TEAMMATES PRODUCE STRONGER RESULTS, PROPELLING A FLYWHEEL OF MEANINGFUL WORK.

- YOU DON'T NEED TO WAIT FOR YOUR MANAGER OR HR TO TELL YOU YOUR PURPOSE. YOU CAN TAP INTO YOUR OWN SENSE OF MEANING BY ARTICULATING YOUR RIPPLE EFFECT, EXPLORING WHAT WOULD HAPPEN IN THE POTENTIAL ABSENCE OF YOUR WORK, AND SEEKING INPUT FROM OTHER PEOPLE ABOUT WHY YOUR WORK MATTERS TO THEM.

Chapter 2

You See What You Look For

"What you see is evidence of what you believe."

—Wayne Dyer

Our brain is hardwired to look for things that match our mental map. The problem is that we're often in the dark about what our mental map actually looks like.

Despite this surface-level oblivion, we are always (consciously and unconsciously) training our brains on what to look for and what to ignore. Our mental framework determines how much attention we pay to particular pieces of the world, which in turn affects how we feel about the world.

Think about the last time you were in the market for a new vehicle. Maybe you were already mostly decided on the ever-reliable Honda Accord. Then, after lots of research, a test drive over the weekend, and weighing the pros and cons, you're pretty positive that's the choice for you.

You pull up to work on Monday and what do you see? Your coworker Phil has an Accord, too! Is it new? No. You just never noticed it, somehow? Time for lunch. How are there FOUR Accords in the Chipotle parking lot? At the end of the day, you pull into your neighborhood, and there's another Accord. This one is in your neighbor's driveway!

Suddenly they're everywhere. It's almost like once the world knew you were considering buying one, they sprung up overnight.

Intellectually, you know you're not the center of the universe . . . so what gives?

The Baader–Meinhof phenomenon refers to the false impression that something happens more frequently than it actually does.[1] This often

33

occurs when we learn something new. Suddenly, this new thing seems to appear more frequently, when in reality it's only our awareness of it that has increased.

That phenomenon happens all the time. When you're after a promotion, your entire LinkedIn feed is people announcing their promotions. When you're considering getting a tattoo, tattoos are everywhere. Your boss made a snide remark about a typo in your proposal. In the last week, you've noticed a typo in every single one of their emails.

This can send us into a spiral of confirmation bias, only seeing the things that support our initial hypothesis. So, if your boss gives you a hard time because of a typo, your brain will see every single typo they make with great clarity. Over time, your mind will have no trouble confirming: your boss is a sloppy, hypocritical jerk who ignores their own failings, yet wakes up every day to mock the innocent errors of others.

If you're looking for evidence for something, you'll find it.

Through a combination of The Baader-Meinhof Phenomenon, confirmation bias, and downright stubbornness, *you will see what you look for* (see Figure 2.1).

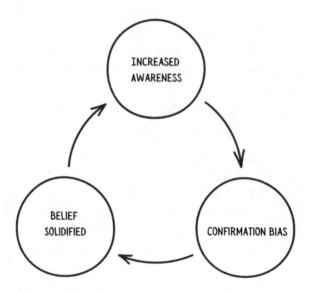

Figure 2.1 Belief cycle.

Mindset is the foundation of self-leadership. If you want to get somewhere you've never been, you have to change the thinking that got you where you are. Consciously challenging your current thoughts is the start.

Here's how a therapist described it to me without the fancy psychological phenomenon names: Think about your recurring thoughts like a deep groove in the soil. You're pushing your wheelbarrow (your life) every day. It's easy to fall back into the same groove. It already exists; it's almost like it's pulling the wheel of your wheelbarrow into it. The more you let your wheelbarrow sink into it, the deeper the groove becomes, and thus, the harder it becomes to forge a new path.

Your brain is going to perform this little mental trickery whether you like it or not. To lead yourself, identifying your existing wheelbarrow ruts is crucial. Knowing your mental rut enables you to recognize when you're slipping back into it. It also makes consciously forging a new path possible.

Let's examine some common mental ruts, why they hold us back, and how we can rewire our thinking.

"Nobody Wants to Work Anymore" and Other Workplace Lies

It's easy to fall into some persuasive (yet untrue) wheelbarrow ruts about work. Before you can start leading yourself, you have to dismantle the beliefs holding you back. Some of these ruts are so widespread that they are as readily accepted as gravity.

The common and widely believed workplace lies are only the tip of the iceberg on the working world's neurological wheelbarrow ruts. When we allow these factually incorrect myths to become our default, we're actually programming our own brains to work against us. Said another way: If you're looking for evidence to prove them true, you'll find it. And you'll have no trouble assimilating with a like-minded pool of grumblers, either.

It's time to let these irksome (and untrue) narratives go. These well-worn grooves in your mind will keep you from putting yourself in the power seat.

"Nobody Wants to Work Anymore"

From CEOs to Facebook trolls, "Nobody wants to work anymore!" became the 2020 cranky-person rallying cry. How true is it?

The numbers tell us that the percentage of the population that's working hasn't changed as dramatically as those decrying collective laziness would lead us to believe. In the United States, the civilian labor force in 2019 was about 163 million. In 2020, it dropped to 161 million (a whopping 1.5%). In 2021, it rose incrementally. In 2022, the US civilian labor force surpassed its previous record, totaling 164 million.[2] Those changes are nearly insignificant.

Are there cases where people, with more time, money, and information, rethought how they approached their careers? Absolutely. Are there particular industries that experienced this more than others? Yes. With a shift to virtual school and a lack of affordable childcare, did some families change their plans? Of course.

But the numbers don't indicate a universal, earth-shaking change suggested by the "nobody wants to work anymore" headlines.

In reality, the deeper truth behind the gripe is:

People don't want to work for assholes *anymore*. People don't want to work for unlivable wages *anymore*. People don't want to work in environments that are toxic *anymore*.

People still want to work; humans have a fundamental drive to make a difference. If disastrous work conditions or poor compensation are overriding that drive . . . well, that's a different (admittedly, less click-baity) headline.

Not only is the "nobody wants to work" sentiment factually inaccurate, it's not even original. If this headline felt oddly familiar to you, it's because you've been seeing it for your whole life.

Paul Fairie, a researcher and instructor at the University of Calgary, traced this narrative as far back as 1894.[3] Here are some of the previous media headlines that brought us to where we are:

- "It almost seems like nobody wants to work anymore and when they do work, they take no pride in what they do." (2006)

- "Nobody wants to work anymore, they want to work in front of a computer and make lots of money." (1999)

- "The trouble is everybody is on relief or a pension; nobody wants to work anymore." (1940)

- "Labor is scarce, high, and very unreliable. None want to work for wages." (1905)

- "With all the mines of the country shut down by strikers, what will the poor editor do for coal next winter? It is becoming apparent that nobody wants to work these hard times." (1894)

Most of these examples come from newspapers, including many publications that still exist today.

More than a century ago, the world's Eeyores had the exact same complaint. When this narrative becomes widespread (like it did in 2020), the awareness of people who don't actually want to work is increased. The "we're hiring" signs around town confirm it. And suddenly, despite a relatively insignificant change to the labor force, the hypothesis *nobody wants to work anymore* has just become valid.

And it doesn't end there. Other workplace lies with the same multi-decade-long history still permeate today's narrative. Do any of these sound familiar?

"This Generation's Young People Are Entitled and Lazy"

In the early 2000s, headline after headline lamented at how difficult the millennials were to work with. These internet-obsessed skinny-jean-wearing buffoons were sure to ruin the world, right? Now, the focus has shifted to Gen Z. All they want to do is make TikToks! They don't even have checkbooks!

Again, not an original narrative. In the 1990s, Gen X was (apparently) as spoiled and unruly as the millennials they (Xers) later complained so much about. Here's what *The Chicago Tribune* wrote about Gen X in 1999: "Theirs is a world saturated by media and popular culture – from the movies to TV and now the Internet – in a way their parents and grandparents never experienced."[4]

The media from the 1960s and 1970s often touted young people (the now Boomers) as spoiled, disrespectful, and paranoid about the government. Headlines from the 1940s and 1950s had their own complaints about the youth of their day (the now 80-year-olds), lamenting that cinemas and motor cars flagged the interest of young people, taking them away from their church and families.

This grumble actually dates back all the way to Hesiod, who in the eighth century BCE famously said:

> I see no hope for the future of our people if they are dependent on frivolous youth of today, for certainly all youth are reckless beyond words . . . When I was young, we were taught to be discreet and respectful of elders, but the present youth are exceedingly wise [disrespectful] and impatient of restraint.[5]

Kids these days! Sheesh!

"Nice Guys Finish Last"

This phrase has likely been muttered by every asshole you've ever worked with. Whether it's used to justify deceiving customers to make a sales goal or undercutting a colleague to steal a promotion, you've undoubtedly heard some jerk use this idiom to defend their behavior.

The original quote, from baseball manager Leo Durocher, was "The nice guys are all over there, in seventh place." He was talking about the 1946 New York Giants – seventh place was next-to-last place in the National League.[6]

The challenge with this one? Nice guys don't actually finish last. It's simply not true, according to the data. Adam Grant famously studied this in *Give and Take*. His extensive research revealed that "givers" (people who give their time and knowledge regularly to help their colleagues) earn more raises and promotions in a wide range of settings.

For example, Grant tells the story of a 19-year-old restaurant worker – an out-and-out giver – who was hired as a waitress but who let the lines of her duties blur to include other restaurant functions. On the basis of the reputation she had earned for her generous working spirit, she was offered and accepted a job managing a new restaurant in Australia. By the age of 26 she was in charge of the chain's restaurants in the whole Asian region. By the age of 32 she was in charge of the whole company. The lady in question was Kat Cole, President of Cinnabon, a billion-dollar brand.

Because of her generous spirit and willingness to go above and beyond, her career accelerated at a rapid pace. The story is the antithesis of "nice guys finish last."

The *nice guys finish last* narrative was also debunked in *The No Asshole Rule*. Author Robert Sutton documents how a prevalence of assholes can upend an entire organization. These people have a ripple effect that ruins motivation, spikes turnover, reduces cooperation, and impairs innovation.

The research and a myriad of individual examples tell us, "Nice guys finish last" isn't true on an individual level or an organizational level.

Of course, there are exceptions. Plenty of assholes seemingly finished "first" (i.e. rich). But it's correlation, not causation. The data suggests that they didn't finish first because they were jerks, they finished first *despite* being jerks. They had breakthrough products, exceptional connections, and in most cases, wealth before they started.

Leading yourself requires that you abandon the notion that being kind means being unsuccessful or unhappy. We also need to let go of another misperception about what constitutes success, like a fully-stacked calendar.

"Important People Are Soooo Busy"

When you ask someone, "How are you?" "Busy!" is the common default response. In many cases, people wear it like a badge of honor.

In TV and movies, important people are always portrayed juggling phone calls and racing to meetings. In a series of experiments, Professor Neeru Paharia of Georgetown University found that study participants unconsciously conclude that busy people are also important and high-status people. Paharia also examined the Twitter feeds of celebrities, finding that rather than boast about their status or wealth, many celebrities want to boast about their lack of time.[7] The prevailing narrative seems to be that busy equates to successful.

It's almost assumed that if you have copious amounts of (or, uh, any) free time, you're not *valuable*. If your calendar isn't full, you must be boring, or undesirable, or useless.

Again, the research tells us, that's not the case. Authors Shawn Achor and Michelle Gielan famously cite this example in *Harvard Business Review*:[8]

> In NBC's *The Office*, while trying to get a promotion from his boss Michael Scott, the awkward and overeager Dwight Schrute shows a spreadsheet documenting that he has never been late and has never taken a day off from work. He does not get the promotion. And that is exactly what the data bears out.
>
> People who took fewer than 10 of their vacation days per year had a 34.6% likelihood of receiving a raise or bonus in a three-year period of time. People who took more than 10 of their vacation days had a 65.4% chance of receiving a raise or bonus.

There's copious amounts of data that proves open calendar space increases productivity, creativity, and overall happiness. Yet, so many of us cling to busyness, many times to our own detriment. So to the people all over LinkedIn bragging about waking up at 5 a.m. to answer emails and being too busy to eat . . . that's not the brag you think it is. Equating busyness with success keeps us from doing the deeper reflection required for leading ourselves. Deciding what kind of self-starter you want to be is unlikely to happen if your life is too busy to think.

Dissolving Your Own Load-Bearing Neural Pathways

It's the voice of your most critical parent, least encouraging teacher, or meanest early-career boss. It lives in the back of your head, dampens your hopes, and looks for validation at every turn.

Maybe your back-of-head voice touts one of the common myths – like nice guys finish last. Maybe yours is (unfortunately) more personal. *You're too loud. You can't focus. You don't try hard enough.*

Or most insidious of all, *you don't deserve it.*

If you've watched any HGTV, you've likely heard the term "load-bearing wall." A trendy designer wants an entirely open concept. The contractor comes in with bad news: the wall between the kitchen and living room is load-bearing. Meaning that wall is holding up the weight of the house (other rooms, upstairs, roof, etc.). It can't come down. Oh no! *Unless . . . we add some support beams.*

The challenge is that's expensive. The load-bearing wall has been there since the house was built. Removing it takes skill, time, and new materials.

Here's an example of the mental version: let's say your parents raised you with the belief that work was a grind. This could've been active on their part; they may have actually said that to you. But in many cases, a load-bearing neural pathway like "work is a grind" is built passively. Your parents come home tired all the time. You hear them complain about their boss. After vacation, they talk about how terrible it's going to be to go back to work. Every Monday, they're in a bad mood. You start to internalize: work sucks.

> It can be helpful to think of our (often incorrect or pessimistic) assumptions as "load-bearing" neural pathways. They're strong, and they hold up a lot of beliefs, decisions, and aspirations. Dismantling them isn't easy.

So, when your first boss treats you badly? You're not surprised. This is what you expected. When work makes you tired and you dread logging on every day? Normal. When you feel like you're not making progress, getting passed over for promotions, or not living up to your potential? Guess there's nothing you can do. Work sucks.

And then, when some wide-eyed newbie walks into your office talking about "purpose" and "making a difference" your internal alarm bells go off. Don't they know? Work sucks! Get over it!

When something (or someone) questions the validity of our load-bearing neural pathways, it's incredibly threatening. If work actually doesn't suck . . . then why have we been sticking it out this way for years? Why

You See What You Look For

did we tolerate a crappy boss or toxic culture? Why didn't we advocate for more? It's much easier to disregard the suggestion of change than to examine a core belief.

The mental version of "removing a load-bearing wall" can be, metaphorically, equally challenging and equally as rewarding as an episode of *Fixer Upper*.

To lead yourself, you must be crystal clear about what's getting in the way of your open concept.

Adding Support Beams

It's impossible to tell yourself "I won't think like that anymore" or "I'm not going to do that again." Millions of failed endeavors fuel the timeless adage: *old habits die hard*.

On HGTV, they don't take the load-bearing wall out and hope for the best. They know that in a few short weeks (if not sooner) the roof is going to collapse on the homeowner. To make the transformation last, they add support beams. You can do the same thing when you're dissolving your own load-bearing neural pathways.

When the negative thought creeps in, you want to have a solid, well-planned defense at the ready. Thinking of it on the spot is too hard.

Here are some examples (see Figure 2.2).

Your counter thought, to combat a negative default, is only going to work if you at least mostly believe it. If you work for a total jerk, your counter thought is not going to be "My boss is the most loving and caring person ever." Your brain will quickly determine: that is a lie.

Even if you find yourself repeating your preemptive, positive thought to yourself with a partial eye roll, over time, it will start to make an impact on your mindset.

If you've ever tried to quit smoking, you know just how important the "substitution" is. There's an entire industry built on it, from patches to gum to lollipops. When you're trying to make a hard mindset change, your brain needs a clear and accessible "instead" rather than just a "don't."

LOAD-BEARING WALL	SUPPORT BEAM
I NEVER HAVE THE RESOURCES	I'M DOING MY BEST WITH WHAT I HAVE
MY BOSS IS A JERK	I SAFEGUARD MY OWN EMOTIONS
OUR PRODUCTS ARE CRAPPY	WE HAVE ROOM FOR IMPROVEMENT AND NEW IDEAS
THIS ORGANIZATION IS SO POLITICAL	I HAVE THE POWER TO BUILD RELATIONSHIPS
I'LL NEVER GET PROMOTED	I DECIDE WHAT'S IMPORTANT TO ME AND HOW TO GET THERE

Figure 2.2 Counter thoughts.

The Risk of Toxic Positivity

Last year I attended an all-hands meeting for a major organization. They'd had a tough year. They got out-innovated in some substantial ways and the economy impacted their industry profoundly. The leadership team wanted the meeting to reinspire their team and galvanize them to turn around the struggling performance.

The CEO kicked off the opening session saying, "What a fantastic year!"

Ummm . . . what? After a year full of layoffs, product failures, missed targets, and salary increases that don't keep up with inflation, the tone of the meeting went from defeated to enraged.

> Consciously focusing on what is going right, dissolving the load-bearing pathways that don't serve you anymore, and pointing your brain to the upside are not synonymous with blind optimism (internal) or toxic positivity (external).

As the team stared down the barrel of even more impossible deliverables, they wondered, were they living a different reality than the C-Suite? What on Earth was this dude talking about? Has no one told him things aren't good?

In that particular meeting, the CEO *was* seeing things that were fantastic. They'd fixed a lot of the product challenges they faced. They'd made a few strategic hires that were already performing. The economy was turning around. Their industry was showing signs of revitalization. Yet, by ignoring the very real struggles his team was facing, his message was received as completely tone-deaf.

Pointing out a potential pitfall does not make you a killjoy. Ignoring challenges doesn't make them go away, it simply ensures you won't be prepared to tackle them.

Holding on to the bright side in the face of hardship is a challenging duality. Yet it's crucial for self-leadership.

Jim Collins addressed this duality in *Good to Great*, when he describes the Stockdale Paradox. Admiral James Stockdale was the highest-ranking officer in a ruthless POW camp ironically dubbed the "Hanoi Hilton" during the Vietnam War. Admiral Stockdale and his fellow prisoners were held hostage for more than seven years, during which they were regularly tortured and often starved. Admiral Stockdale is widely credited with keeping his team alive, in body and spirit.

During an interview,[9] when Jim Collins asked Admiral Stockdale how he held on to hope in such bleak circumstances, Stockdale said, "I never lost faith in the end of the story. I never doubted not only that I would get out, but also that I would prevail in the end."

When Collins asked Stockdale, "Who didn't make it out?" Stockdale said bluntly: The optimists. The optimists, Stockdale says, were the prisoners who kept thinking, we're going to be out by Thanksgiving, then, Thanksgiving would come and go. Then they'd say, we'll get out by Christmas, and Christmas would come and go. Eventually, they died of a broken heart.

He elaborated, saying, "You must never confuse faith that you will prevail in the end – which you can never afford to lose – with the discipline to confront the most brutal facts of your current reality, whatever they might be."

I hope what you're facing pales in comparison to being a prisoner of war. If Admiral Stockdale can live this duality in that environment, I'm sure you can muster up some of it in your corporate job.

When It (Inevitably) Still Goes to Shit

Our brains gloss over all the times our takeout order is correct, all the days we wake up without a stuffy nose, and every person who uses their turn signal on the road. Training your brain to notice how often things are going "right" helps the rough patches feel more insignificant. Which statistically speaking, they are.

According to the National Science Foundation, an average person has about 12 000–60 000 thoughts per day. Of those, 80% are negative and 95% are repetitive thoughts.[10]

When you're actively trying to rewire yourself, a snide remark or a rough day can feel like a personal affront. Self-starters are not immune to intrusive thoughts. They experience rough patches, setbacks, and derailments. Each person battles their own unhelpful beliefs and assumptions.

If you're searching for evidence that your boss doesn't care, your spouse is rude, or your career is off track . . . you'll find it. If you're searching for things to be grateful for, small moments of joy, and opportunities for connection, you'll find those, too.

There's a tricky duality between reframing normal annoyances while also acknowledging you shouldn't continually put up with garbage, and you should never tolerate abuse. Here are some examples, in Figure 2.3.

The annoying category, and to some degree the garbage category, is workable. Not ideal, sure, but you can finesse it, and even minimize it. We'll talk more about how in Part III of this book.

For now, know this: The more you expect it, prepare for it, and manage it, the less of an impact these derailers will have on your work experience. When you let the annoyance consume your brain, or if you convince yourself the annoyance is actually garbage or abuse, the more power you give it.

ANNOYING	GARBAGE	ABUSE
YOUR BOSS CHANGES THEIR MIND A LOT AND DOESN'T GIVE CLEAR DIRECTIONS	YOUR BOSS CONTINUALLY UNDOES YOUR WORK OR DOESN'T USE YOUR WORK WITHOUT EXPLAINING WHY	YOUR BOSS CALLS YOU AN IDIOT FOR NOT READING THEIR MIND ALL THE TIME
A COWORKER REFERS TO THE WORK YOU DID ALONE AS A "TEAM EFFORT"	A COWORKER KNOWINGLY TAKES FULL CREDIT FOR YOUR IDEA IN A MEETING	A COWORKER DOUBLES DOWN AND TELLS YOUR BOSS YOU DIDN'T COME UP WITH THIS IDEA AND YOU NEVER COME UP WITH IDEAS
YOUR NEW JOB DESCRIPTION LEFT OUT A FEW ADMINISTRATIVE TASKS YOU'RE NOW FINDING OUT ARE YOUR RESPONSIBILITY	YOUR NEW JOB DESCRIPTION DESCRIBED THE CULTURE AS COLLABORATIVE AND PURPOSE-DRIVEN; YOUR FIRST FEW MONTHS WOULD INDICATE OTHERWISE...	YOUR NEW JOB DESCRIPTION WAS NOT ACCURATE AT ALL AND THE COMPENSATION IS NOT WHAT WAS DISCUSSED IN THE HIRING PROCESS

Figure 2.3 Annoying, garbage, or abuse.

If you want to lead yourself in the long haul, don't let a bad day steal your month. Don't let a bad job steal your career. And don't let a bad boss steal your peace.

REMEMBER

- IF YOU'RE LOOKING FOR EVIDENCE OF SOMETHING, YOU'LL FIND IT. INTENTIONALLY POINT YOUR BRAIN TO WHAT YOU WANT TO SEE (MEANING, PURPOSE, JOY, AND OPPORTUNITIES).

- DON'T FALL VICTIM TO FALSE NARRATIVES LIKE "NOBODY WANTS TO WORK ANYMORE" OR "NICE GUYS FINISH LAST." CHALLENGE YOUR OWN ASSUMPTIONS ABOUT WHAT WORK CAN BE.

- TELLING YOURSELF "I WON'T THINK LIKE THAT ANYMORE" OR "I'M NOT GOING TO DO THAT AGAIN" ISN'T ENOUGH. INSTEAD, WHEN THE NEGATIVE THOUGHT CREEPS IN, YOU WANT TO HAVE A WELL-PLANNED COUNTER THOUGHT AT THE READY. THINKING OF IT ON THE SPOT IS TOO HARD. FOR EXAMPLE, INSTEAD OF RUMINATING ON THE THOUGHT, "THIS ORGANIZATION IS SO POLITICAL," COUNTER WITH "I HAVE THE POWER TO BUILD RELATIONSHIPS."

Chapter 3

Quiet Fear

"Fear cuts deeper than swords."
> —George R.R. Martin, *A Game of Thrones*

When you are about to give a big presentation, pitch an idea, or do something courageous, the onslaught of mental "what ifs" will have no problem keeping you awake at night. What if it's awful, what if they hate me, what if I blow it and never get another chance?

Our not-always-helpful brain tends to default to the negative "what ifs" when we make ourselves vulnerable and put ourselves out there. The potential shame of failure can be more initially jarring than the possibility of the upside.

Let us be honest; for all their talk of driving innovation, being nimble, and taking risks, most organizations (and most bosses) do not leap with glee when someone starts doing things differently. This part of the book is about your mindset. In Part II, we are going to be talking about things you can start doing differently. That's why we have to get the lingering fears out of your brain first.

> One of the challenges of leading yourself is to overcome that nagging little voice telling you to wait for approval, ask permission, or at the very least, avoid doing anything outside the norm that might draw attention to yourself.

Our quest to avoid risk is primitive. In *The Gift of Fear*, Gavin De Becker writes, "Nature's greatest accomplishment, the human brain, is never more efficient or invested than when its host is at risk."[1]

Organizational psychologists will often refer to this survival instinct as our "lizard brain." Technically, it's a metaphor for the amygdala, the part of your limbic system that is responsible for your emotions. Your amygdala assesses the situation and, based on the level of perceived risk, will almost immediately tell you to fight, flee, or freeze.

Intellectually, we may know fumbling a sales call or missing a deadline is not the equivalent of being eaten by a bear, even if it feels that way at the moment.

Self-starters who take the reins of leading themselves accept risk as inevitable. Whether it's joining a new startup, heading up a special project, or just asking a tough question in a meeting, they know that risk can fuel their progress.

Easier said than done, at least for me. To overcome fear (when you know you are making a reasonable sound decision and you are not about to die), you'll have to convince your lizard brain to temporarily chill out.

The Upside

What if you could walk into a room and share your ideas with full confidence? What if you could give (or receive) feedback without awkwardly stumbling through it? What if you could raise your hand for the big opportunity without the gnawing feeling that someone else would be a better choice?

You can, once you learn how to manage your own brain.

I'm not suggesting you trick your brain into making blindly optimistic decisions; you must accurately assess what risk is worth taking. For a risk to be worth it, the upside should be substantial. The challenge is that the upside is rarely as blatantly obvious as the risk; it's subtle and more nuanced. Let us look at some examples in Figures 3.1–3.3.

In these three scenarios, the upside *generally* outweighs the risk. But it's not what our brain instinctively latches onto first.

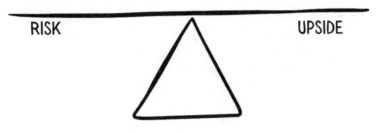

GIVING A PRESENTATION TO THE BOARD

YOU FUMBLE THROUGH SOME PARTS AND DON'T FULLY LAND IT. (THE BOARD THINKS IT WAS BLAH AND MOVES ON WITH THEIR LIFE, FINDING THE CLARIFICATION THEY NEED ELSEWHERE.)

PRESENTATION GOES GREAT, LOTS OF KUDOS FROM YOUR BOSS. (YOU MAKE A GREAT IMPRESSION ON THE MOST SENIOR LEADERS IN YOUR ORGANIZATION AND YOUR BOSS IS THRILLED.)

RISK   UPSIDE

Figure 3.1   Board presentation risk versus reward.

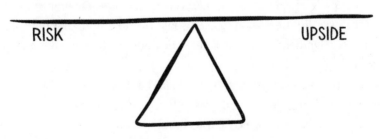

BRINGING A NEW IDEA TO YOUR BOSS

THEY HATE YOUR IDEA. (IF YOU'VE DONE YOUR HOMEWORK, AND HAVE A GOOD RELATIONSHIP WITH YOUR BOSS, THIS ISN'T LIKELY TO SET YOU BACK MORE THAN A DAY, IF AT ALL.)

THEY LOVE YOUR IDEA. (THIS COULD PROPEL THE RELATIONSHIP WITH YOUR BOSS EVEN FURTHER AND HELP GARNER YOUR REPUTATION AS A STRATEGIC, CREATIVE THINKER.)

RISK   UPSIDE

Figure 3.2   New idea risk versus reward.

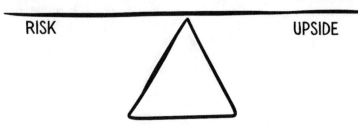

DELIVERING TOUGH FEEDBACK TO A COLLEAGUE

THEY DISCOUNT YOUR FEEDBACK AND YOUR RELATIONSHIP IS TEMPORARILY DAMAGED. (IF YOU'VE DELIVERED THE FEEDBACK COURTEOUSLY, WITH POSITIVE INTENT, THIS LIKELY HAS MORE TO DO WITH THEM THAN YOU.)

YOUR CHALLENGING CONVERSATION MAKES YOUR COLLEAGUE'S PROJECT BETTER. (THEY'RE MORE CONFIDENT NOW, MORE LIKELY TO SUCCEED, AND THEY KNOW THEY CAN COUNT ON YOU TO GIVE IT TO THEM STRAIGHT.)

RISK UPSIDE

Figure 3.3 Tough feedback risk versus reward.

Dorie Clark, the author of *The Long Game: How to Be a Long-Term Thinker in a Short-Term World,* said something that stuck with me on the topic of overcoming fear.

She said, "People often tend to systematically overestimate the level of threat in certain situations. For example, if someone is afraid to be authentic at work, they may say things like 'that's not tolerated here.' And when you dig deeper into it and ask them – you must've seen examples where someone tried to be authentic and got smashed down, right? They almost never have. There's hardly ever any evidence. People are imagining scenarios where they get fired or ostracized or some horrible thing happens if they ask for an assignment, push back on something, or try to make a change. It's often simply not true."

If you find yourself starting to think, "What if it goes terribly and they hate it," interrupting that thought cycle before it spirals is crucial. To lead yourself, you must actively point your brain to the payoff.

Putting yourself out there, being more proactive, and taking initiative where you see opportunity requires courage.

For example, before your pitch, you may start to think, "What if everyone laughs at my idea?" Interrupt your thought cycle with the prospect of "What if it goes awesome and everyone loves it?" It will feel uncomfortable to think this at first; it's a new thought pattern and mentally awkward.

Articulating the upside, in detail, enables you to be more confident and courageous before bold action. The risk is still there; it's just not monopolizing your brain space.

Deciding When to Go for It

In the movie *We Bought a Zoo*, there's a scene when the father (Benjamin Mee, who bought a zoo) is giving advice to his teenage son. The son had just opened up to his father about a girl he liked, who he did not have the courage to talk to.

His father encouraged him to make a move, saying, "You know, sometimes all you need is 20 seconds of insane courage. Just literally 20 seconds of just embarrassing bravery. And I promise you, something great will come of it."

I adore the sentiment of that line, though I do think it could've gone without the impossible promise of certainty.

Deciding when to demonstrate your 20 seconds of insane courage is challenging in the corporate world. We know growth begins at the end of our comfort zone, but stepping too far out of your comfort zone can trigger a fight or flight response (or at least an uncomfortable conversation with your boss).

For example, I'm not going to have a growth experience if I volunteer to build a jet engine. I'm going to have an anxiety attack. I would not know where to start or even what materials I need. I do not have any informed support system to help me when things inevitably get challenging. If I somehow manage to build something that makes its way into an actual jet, the risk for civilian life is huge.

However, I would have a growth experience if speaking to a team of CEOs or confronting a colleague about an ongoing problem. Am I going to be nervous beforehand? Yes. Is the potential payoff worth it? In my case, yes.

When you are deciding when to quiet the fear and go for growth, you don't have to make the decision blindly. It helps to examine the varying factors that contribute to your success individually. Only one of those factors is your actual skill. When you're assessing whether you should muster up your courage, consider these prompts:

- Do you have the skills to achieve this?
- Do you have the resources (time, money, brain space) to achieve this?
- Do you have the support of (ideally skilled) people?
- Is the risk at least a little bit less significant than the upside?
- Are you OK with failing? Not, will you like failing. Of course, you will not. But will you be mostly OK?

You do not need to answer a resounding "yes" to each of those prompts. Three out of five is typically enough. That last one – are you OK with failing – tends to be the zinger for even the most ambitious self-starters.

Even if you muster all of your courage to go for something, you might get shut down. There will be inevitable instances when your brain says "Grow!" and your boss says "No!"

If you are dialed into the purpose of your organization, you are likely seeing opportunities for growth and improvement. Your boss may not be receptive to those at first. People who lead themselves are exceptional at identifying opportunities to step up within the boundaries of their current work *without* pissing off their boss.

Walking through those categories with your boss can help. At first mention, your boss might not see the support system you have or the potential upside. They (like all humans) will zoom in on the risk and the possibility of failure *first*. When they see your rationale, they might become your biggest cheerleader (or at least grumbly allow you to move forward).

For example, you may suggest that you head up some customer focus groups. Your boss is skeptical. What would you even say to them? When would you do it? What if customers do not respond well to the ask?

You can present your case by addressing some of these factors proactively. Answering these questions, before your boss asks them, enables you to quiet *their* fear (and it increases the odds they'll say yes).

This chapter is called "quiet fear," not "silence fear." There will always be a risk-averse little lizard in the back of your brain. It serves a purpose. When he rears his pointy little head, you can thank him for his service, and assure him you are not actually in grave danger.

Letting the lizard get too loud and allowing the voice of fear to overtake your aspirations does not always happen in one big moment, like turning down a job. It happens in the small moments, like deciding not to speak up in a meeting, not raising your hand to champion a project, or not asking for a meeting with someone you want to know. It's a thousand tiny choices to stay on the sidelines that, over time, will (incorrectly) convince you that *the sidelines are where you belong.*

> It's helpful to remind yourself that there's risk in staying the course, too. Sometimes not changing is the biggest risk of all, even if it feels like the safest bet at the moment.

There's a quote from Carson McCullers that sums this up perfectly: "We are torn between nostalgia for the familiar and an urge for the foreign and strange. As often as not, we are homesick most for the places we have never known."

Today, you may feel tempted to stay within the boundaries of your neatly defined job, dutifully delivering what's in your scope, shepherding your mind away from any of that "other stuff." It does not hurt today; it likely will not tomorrow. Yet, as years pass by, your heart will start to yearn, wondering what would've happened if you went for it.

Own Your Potential

There's an interesting phenomenon that happens when you are applying for a new job: your potential comes to the forefront of your mind. The interview process forces your brain to explore what your future could look like. Even if you don't fully plan on leaving your current role, once your vision for yourself changes, it's hard to go back.

Laura Gassner Otting makes this point beautifully in her TEDx talk, *Why doesn't success bring happiness?*

She says, "Do you know why internal candidates always leave if they don't get the job? Because the very process of interviewing for the bigger job means that once they saw themselves in this new way, even if for a moment, they couldn't unsee themselves in this new way."

Once you see the possibility of something – a new job, a new career, even your internal project taking off – you cannot unsee it. Whether it's a new role, filling out a Request for Proposal, or applying to give a TED talk, allowing your brain to sit in the "what could be" stage helps you reconnect with possibility.

Too often, we cover our eyes, bury our heads into our to-do lists, and forget what's possible for our lives. We cost the world, and ourselves, so much when we lose sight of our potential.

Leading yourself is about recognizing your own potential. You do not need to wait on your boss, or their boss, or your next job to see what's possible for you.

Having said that, recognizing your true potential comes with both promise and heartbreak. Promise because you know what's possible, and heartbreak, because you know what's possible.

REMEMBER

- THERE WILL ALWAYS BE A RISK-AVERSE LITTLE LIZARD IN THE BACK OF YOUR BRAIN. IT SERVES A PURPOSE; YOU CAN THANK HIM FOR HIS SERVICE AND ASSURE HIM THAT YOU'RE NOT ACTUALLY IN GRAVE DANGER.

- OUR NOT-ALWAYS-HELPFUL LIZARD BRAIN DEFAULTS TO NEGATIVE "WHAT IFS." THE POTENTIAL OF SHAME OF FAILURE IS MORE INITIALLY JARRING THAN THE POSSIBILITY OF THE UPSIDE. YOU CAN QUIET FEAR BY ARTICULATING THE UPSIDE IN DETAIL. FOR EXAMPLE, BEFORE YOUR PITCH, YOU MAY START TO THINK "WHAT IF EVERYONE LAUGHS AT MY IDEA?" INTERRUPT YOUR THOUGHT CYCLE WITH THE PROSPECT OF, "WHAT IF IT GOES AWESOME AND EVERYONE LOVES IT?" IT MIGHT FEEL AWKWARD AT FIRST, BUT THE ABILITY TO ARTICULATE THE UPSIDE WILL SERVE YOU FOR YOUR WHOLE LIFE.

Chapter 4

Embrace Change and Uncertainty

"If you want something you've never had, you must be willing to do something you've never done."

—A quote regularly and falsely attributed to
Thomas Jefferson . . . which is too bad, since it's a nice quote

Is AI taking your job? Maybe, maybe not. Are you going to be replaced by a robot? Maybe, maybe not. The future of technology certainly won't be determined by your personal level of anxiety around it.

Your fretfulness also won't determine your place in a reorg. It won't make a difference in how threatening that new competitor turns out to be. It's certainly not going to impact how much your crypto is worth. Yet, here we are (I'm with you on this) *fretful*. Despite knowing that anxiety and worry are not helping us, we often find ourselves mired in it.

You have no doubt heard the adage: *change is the only constant*. It's an inconvenient truth, never more poignant than now.

Human beings are OK with change (sometimes) . . . when we are prepared for it, in control of it, and see a win for ourselves at the end. People bring change on themselves voluntarily all the time, like getting married, leaving a toxic job, or traveling to another country. Those changes are exciting.

Yet, change in the corporate world can often feel *exhausting,* especially en masse. As uncertainty remains, return-to-office plans stumble, and organizations continue to overuse the word "pivot," it's easy to feel depleted.

In one of her courses, Cassandra Worthy, a fellow author and LinkedIn Learning Instructor, said something once that really stuck with me: "What

> Leading yourself
> requires you to not only
> tolerate change but
> embrace it.

if we viewed change as an opportunity for growth?"[1]

As a self-admitting control freak, I admire the gusto Cassandra brings into the unknown. She defines her trademark Change Enthusiasm as, "A mindset that when practiced, presents a sense of excitement for every change challenge. It is a mindset which enables those who practice it the ability to see the value of change, thereby quickly engaging in the opportunity to evolve in the face of frustration."

She wasn't always that way, though. Which means there's hope for the rest of us. In her book, *Change Enthusiasm*, Cassandra talks openly about the difficult experience of working for a company during a billion-dollar merger: "I was so frustrated at the end of nearly every day that I began actively looking for a way to transfer out of the business and even quit the company – a company I had not long before loved and envisioned contributing to for decades to come."

In frustration, Cassandra phoned a senior-level mentor, venting about how tough of a time she was having and how seriously she was considering quitting the company. Her mentor offered some candid advice, "Cassandra, you can either get bitter or you can get better. It's your choice."

Cassandra chose the latter.

With a revised view, Cassandra successfully navigated the daily change and uncertainty, viewing it as an opportunity for growth. Her new mindset had a major impact on her career trajectory. She thrived and went on to navigate another, even more significant merger several years later. These massive changes weren't without annoyance, frustration, or even anger. Those were still present; Cassandra just made sure they weren't the loudest thoughts in her head. They were supporting actors in her story of confidence and growth.

When we aren't in full control, bitterness is the tempting path to take. Bitter that we can't unilaterally make the decision, cut the loss, or chart a new path. Yet, when you proactively choose to view change as an opportunity for growth, you up the odds that you'll navigate the change successfully.

Optimism is contagious and confidence opens doors. Even more importantly than the work win, there's a personal win. Truly believing in an upside, no matter how messy, safeguards you, to some degree, against the psychological and physiological pains that come with fear.

This Is Your Chance

As we've worked through finding more purpose in our existing job, shifting our lens toward more positive experiences, quieting our fears, and making peace with change, I hope you can see how making these mental shifts provides you with a strong base, one that is vastly different from the way most people experience their jobs.

With clarity of purpose, an ability to point your own lens, and the skill to work past workplace fears, you can handle things that cause other people to get derailed. This is a crucial foundation because with the accelerated rate of change we each face, sometimes it feels like your day is getting hijacked before it even starts. Without a solid base, you're not prepared to deal with changes and uncertainty. If you're finding yourself constantly bombarded with changes and "urgent" to-dos and interruptions, you're not alone.

A new report was recently unveiled by German Think Tank Next Work Innovation, highlighting interruptions at work statistics. The study found that employees in knowledge-intensive professions are interrupted an average of 15 times per hour. This equates to one interruption every four minutes.[2] The financial impact of that is profound. The emotional impact is equally if not more frightening.

Leading yourself would be a lot easier if you didn't have to deal with other people. But like it or not, your reality is filled with people who have their own demands and deliverables. When you're leading yourself, and you work for or with literally anyone, odds are, you'll be interrupted. Your challenge is to make sure that an interruption, change in direction, or "pivot" doesn't derail you.

That's where the "this is my chance" practice comes in. I first learned of this practice from Tessa Romero, a mindset coach who focuses on motherhood. If you've ever been around a small child, you know the interruptions are constant, maybe even more so than in corporate America.

The "this is my chance" practice prompts you to mentally reframe whatever was thrust upon you (a change, an urgent action item, etc.) into an opportunity.

Imagine you're the parent of a six-year-old. It's the holidays and you've planned a very festive Saturday. You've thoughtfully lined up pictures with Santa, decorating the tree, and a tour of the neighborhood Christmas lights. You made sure the outfit was clean, the ornaments were out of the attic, and the car had gas. You're really looking forward to it. Saturday morning rolls around. Your kid climbs into your bed at 4 a.m. and pukes.

It is easy at that moment to feel frustrated; you had put a lot of work into preparing for what you thought would be a great day. You're disappointed and sad.

Yet you can't control the stomach flu; you can only control your response. The reframe would be, "This is my chance to slow down and lean into what my child needs. This is my chance to throw on a Christmas movie and make soup instead. This is my chance to show up in a way I'm proud of."

In that scenario, you took your brain from being annoyed at the things outside of your control (stomach flu) to being empowered about the things inside your control (how you show up). Using the mental jogger of "this is my chance" you reframed the interruption, a change, curveball, etc., into an opportunity.

It's easy to see the shift in that example, because who would be mad at a kid for getting sick? They didn't do it on purpose. Practicing "this is my chance" is easier when you unconditionally love the person doing the interrupting. We don't generally have the same adoration for our coworkers or our boss. Yet, the "this is my chance" practice still works.

Here are a few examples in Figure 4.1.

I've personally been practicing this for a year. It felt awkward and clunky at first. Some of my "this is my chance" reframes were accompanied by an eye roll. Then it got easier. The practice radiated into my work, and the difference it's made in my own resilience is shocking.

Of course, taken to the extreme, this practice can lead you into being an absolute doormat. We are not responding to unsafe working conditions

I HAVE TO ANSWER THOSE URGENT QUESTIONS.	THIS IS MY CHANCE TO ADD MORE CLARITY AND MAKE SURE WE'RE ALIGNED.
AI IS SO SCARY, I WONDER IF IT WILL TAKE MY JOB.	THIS IS MY CHANCE TO LEARN NEW TOOLS AND BRING MY UNIQUELY HUMAN SKILLS TO THE FORE.
UGH. MY BOSS JUST POSTPONED OUR 1-1.	THIS IS MY CHANCE TO REFLECT ON WHAT I PLANNED TO BRING UP; MAYBE THERE'S SOMETHING I MISSED.
I CANNOT BELIEVE WE HAD ANOTHER DELAY. MY CUSTOMERS ARE GOING TO BE SO PISSED.	THIS IS MY CHANCE TO BE PROACTIVE & BUILD MY CUSTOMER RELATIONSHIPS THROUGH A ROUGH MOMENT.
I DO NOT HAVE TIME FOR ANOTHER PROJECT TO BE ADDED ONTO MY PLATE.	THIS IS MY CHANCE TO GET BETTER AT DELEGATING AND OUTSOURCING.

Figure 4.1 This is my chance examples.

with "This is my chance to be brave!" We are not responding to the billionth restructure and salary clawback with "This is my chance to budget more aggressively!"

Remember the "normal versus annoying versus garbage" chart in Chapter 2? Do not continually tolerate garbage and never tolerate abuse. The "this is my chance" practice is a mental reframe used for the normal annoyances every job has; it's not a pass for cruel behavior.

We'll talk more about reducing the volume of interruptions and fending off false urgency in Chapter 6. For the interruptions that are inevitable, having the four words (this is my chance) at the forefront of your mind gives you a shortcut to bring your best self to an unanticipated situation.

> "This is my chance" works in the micro (like dealing with daily interruptions). It also works in the macro, like embracing generative AI and other emerging technologies.

> There's a personal, emotional win for embracing change. There's also a hugely practical career win. The ability to operate in the face of change and uncertainty is tremendously helpful in keeping your own sanity at work. It also makes you look really good to the people who are in charge.

When I was in college, my favorite professor, Professor Craig Sender, used the expression "evolve or die" probably a thousand times during a single semester. I say that lovingly. It's a poignant reminder that has stuck with me for well over a decade. I find myself coming back to it when I'm tempted to dig my heels into the sand of the present.

When I last talked to him, I asked him about AI, and if his current students were afraid of its impact on their field (communication). Here's what he said: "What I tell my students – who are scared to death that their skillset will become obsolete – is that in the near term, you won't lose your job to AI, but you will lose your job to someone who knows how to use AI. Start using and get comfortable with technology. Don't fear it and don't run away. I remember when we started using the internet at work. I remember thinking, this makes my job so much easier! Things that used to take hours now take minutes! This is the same evolution. If I'm hiring someone, I want someone who isn't afraid of technology. I want someone who is embracing it."

Instead of wishing you could be more optimistic or resilient, force yourself to do it, even if you roll your eyes. Soon enough, it won't be forced. This is your chance.

Lose Your Attachment to Sunk Costs

The internet is filled with stories of resilience. JK Rowling, who wrote the Harry Potter series, was rejected by 12 publishers before finally landing it. The founder of Uber was turned down by Mark Cuban when he asked for an investment.

Those leaders *prevailed*. They pushed through rejection, doubt, and setbacks, and they *never gave up*. But should those anecdotes serve as grounds for you to send a tenth follow-up email or try, yet again, to organize the internal server? Probably not.

The messiness behind those examples (and countless other LinkedIn hype posts) is that JK Rowling and the founder of Uber gave up lots of times, just not on the ideas they're now famous for. JK Rowling started two novels, but scrapped them both without finishing them, declaring them to have been "rubbish." Travis Kalanick, an original Uber founder, had a previous startup called Red Swoosh that landed him in hot water with the IRS.

Both of them, and every other leader touted in "resilient" headlines, knew when to call it quits and move on to the next thing. What ultimately catapults individuals to the Achievement Hall of Fame is rarely the first thing they try.

The long-touted advice of "never give up" should have an asterisk on it. No one wants to spend decades of their mental energy pursuing something ultimately fruitless in the name of "never giving up."

Leaders, both formal and informal, give up all the time. It's impossible to be efficient with your time if you unwaveringly commit to everything you start. The nuance is to recognize *when* to give up, and in some cases, help your boss come to that realization, too.

Leading yourself doesn't mean banging your head against a wall forever. Unfortunately, ambitious people often let sunk costs get the best of them, giving up way too late. When you've already invested your time and brainpower, it's difficult to accept that it's not working. Yet, in most instances, investing more time and thinking won't change the inevitable.

I was talking with my friend Vanessa, who heads up marketing for a boutique clothing brand. She was telling me about a new influencer program they launched. Vanessa vetted tons of potential influencers, personally shipped them products, worked with them on creating content, and pulled together an editorial calendar. It was a huge undertaking. And it wasn't working.

When Vanessa dug deeper, she realized a lot of the influencers were buying followers and likes on their posts. The engagement wasn't real, and because it wasn't real, the campaign was driving $0 in sales. Vanessa was very upset, lamenting to me about how much time and energy she put into trying to make the strategy successful.

In a meeting with her boss, the COO, Vanessa made the bold suggestion to cut their losses and stop influencer marketing.

It would have been easy for her to get defensive or tout that brand awareness, even if it's not driving sales, is worth something. She could've pleaded for more time or another round of influencers. But she didn't. She took the L and she moved on, with exponentially more respect from her boss than had she clung to something fruitless.

Great leaders fail, but they do it fast, and then they move on. Their failures can be painful but they're often not public. That's why it's so easy to think giving up isn't something that resilient and successful people do.

No one is publicly touting "I wasted too much time on this!" or "My gut told me it wouldn't work and I didn't listen!"

With an eye to the future possibility (not the historic investment), be realistic with yourself about how likely success is to appear in the final hour. How are you going to change what you've been doing? If you don't change, and the circumstances don't change, the result likely won't either.

Embracing giving up and diving back into the perils of uncertainty after you thought you had it figured out is hard. Wishing that you called it quits a year (or more) earlier is worse.

Avoiding the Ick of "Startup Culture"

You can't use phrases like "embracing uncertainty" or "change agent" without addressing the culture of startups.

Startups have an exceptional track record of propelling change and upending longstanding industries. The Unicorns achieved their status by innovating quickly and oftentimes avoiding some of the red tape and hierarchical sludge that slows down their big-company competitors.

Sometime in the mid-2000s, large organizations got the idea that they should "act like a startup" to move faster and innovate more boldly.

While spurring innovation and embracing uncertainty is a well-intended idea, some organizations took the idea of "act like a startup" to be synonymous with "be unorganized and don't offer health insurance."

While organizational change is inevitable, constant chaos at the hands of powerful executives is not. Today, the messaging of innovation and disruption is still often misconstrued to justify budget cuts, poor planning, or even malicious practices.

The following is how the distinction between true startup culture versus poor planning or a misallocation of resources often plays out. Green flags indicate an organization (no matter the size) is harnessing the best of the fast-moving, innovative startup culture. Red flags are (obviously) the opposite. These signs suggest that an organization isn't disrupting for good. They're evoking start-up culture as a cloak for bad behavior. Here's how you can tell the difference:

The Lens on Innovation

Green flag: The noblest of startups are bound together by a desire to improve their customers and the world. That emotional fuel carries them through setbacks or other restraints. These startups innovate with a lens on how they can make an impact and scale their business. They know their customers exceptionally well and are always striving to serve them in bolder, more effective ways.

Red flag: You've undoubtedly heard your share of executives touting that capitalism breeds innovation. But have you ever bought paper towels? Twelve rolls somehow equals 24 because the package says so. Innovation through the lens of doing *less* for customers is not how "scrappy startups" operate. The *why* behind doing new things is the most important factor to consider when you're deciding whether to embrace change. Shrinkflation (reducing the package size but not the price) is not a sustainable practice and supposed savvy marketing (like paper towel math) is annoying. Saving on costs or streamlining processes are necessary, but those factors shouldn't be the organizational-wide eternal narrative.

The Authority of Decision-Making

Green flag: Startups are able to move quickly because they empower middle managers and individual contributors to make decisions and execute new ideas. These organizations accept an inevitable rate of misfire in exchange for speed. Autonomy and authority are why so many people love working at startups.

Red flag: Leadership wants new ideas . . . until they get them. Fast decisions *and* executive-sign-off-on-everything are mutually exclusive. Having both is not possible. An organization or leader that champions speed and agility should not be the sole keeper of the word "go."

The Internal Infrastructure

Green flag: A payroll specialist is not generally an early hire in a new business. Neither are learning and development teams, specialized IT experts, or other internal resources often found at larger organizations. Early team members assume they'll be DIY-ing things beyond their job description because if they don't, no one will. This should change with time and scale.

Red flag: From payroll and benefits to setting up your laptop, you're on your own. Corporate is handling things on a forever "case by case" basis. Hundreds if not thousands of employees who are confused and undersupported in basic operations is not a standard in "startup culture."

The Available Resources

Green flag: Early-day startups are generally quite lean in the resources available. They often seek funding from outside investors and have a short runway of cash. Because money is tight, spending it takes careful consideration. Lavish retreats or unlimited tech stacks aren't typically available. The ROI is a filter on every investment. Money is spent, but it's done so scrupulously.

Red flag: Doing more with less . . . then less . . . then even less! In a tough economic climate or through an industry change, budget cuts are inevitable. Even layoffs can be the (unfortunately) right business decision. Yet, when things trend one-way year after year, especially if that's not the industry norm, your eyebrow should raise. Lacking resources because you truly don't have cash and lacking resources because you're trying to drive a tenth of a point to share price (and exec bonuses) are two very different things.

The Flow of Money

Green flag: Another reason startups tend to have a recruiting advantage is the potential (though not guarantee) of big money. Getting in early with the right organization can mean a significant financial return. Early employees are often offered performance bonuses and even equity. Sometimes this comes in exchange for a lower salary. It's a dice roll many, especially startup veterans, choose to make.

Red flag: *Someone* is making money, just not you. This became really obvious when a large percentage of the workforce was forced to work remotely in 2020. You Zoomed in from your living room and the CEO Zoomed in from their hot tub . . . which overlooks the ocean, only to tell you times are tough, and cuts must be made. If your salary isn't keeping up with inflation and the executive team is flying private, your company isn't scrappy; they're selfish.

Good companies go through hard times. But some companies are *always* in a "hard time," failing to recognize that constant chaos is actually their resting state. Those red flags are extra-bright red if the organization is sizeable and with significant history.

Adapting to change is a hallmark of someone who can lead themselves. Resilience matters and seeing change as an opportunity for growth is a lifelong mindset that can transform your career. Yet spotting the red flags behind a change can save you massive headaches and heartache.

A baseline level of change will be constant; organizational mayhem shouldn't be.

Don't Wait for Everything to Be "Settled"

I was working with a sales team in a fast-growing startup. The team was facing an onslaught of changes. Their product was evolving substantially, they were entering new markets, and on top of that, a new Chief Revenue Officer was on the horizon. Literally nothing was "settled."

During all this change, most of the sales team was (unsurprisingly) having a hard time meeting quota. Customers were asking lots of questions, territories were changing, and a palpable level of anxiety radiated through the sales Slack channel.

Yet a small handful of top performers were still performing. They answered their customers' questions to the best of their abilities, they sold the products they had available to them, and – most importantly – they maintained confidence that they'd figure it out.

I was impressed and honestly a little surprised. Given the scope of the transformation on the horizon, compartmentalizing the constant changes enough to be fully engaged in your daily role can be a herculean mental effort, especially when comp plans and territories are changing, too.

In a series of interviews, I dug deeper to understand the distinctions between the reps who were selling and the reps who were mentally consumed by the volume of changes.

In my conversations with the team, I started to pick up on an important distinction. Most of the team was waiting for certainty. While those who were still performing accepted that certainty was never coming. Sure, some decisions might be made, and offerings will become clearer. But it would never be certain.

One star performer summed up his stance with "I don't know what my job is going to look like in three months from now. But I know what it looks like today."

At first blush, that might read as a disempowered "there's nothing I can do anyway!" grumble. It wasn't. It was the opposite. The tone was confident and empowering. The top performers weren't giving up in the face of change nor were they mentally willing themselves to deny it was happening.

If you're always waiting for change to be "over" . . . you'll always be waiting.

I've fallen victim to the "wait for it to be settled" trap myself, in various roles. The same dynamic plays out in our personal lives, too. Do any of these sound familiar?

Instead, these stand-out reps were accepting an ever-present volume of change, and within that context, they empowered themselves to operate *anyway*. They controlled the controllable, and as a result, drastically outperformed their peers.

- I'm going to wait until we renovate our kitchen to start entertaining.

- I'll show up to a class reunion once I drop 10 pounds.

- We can't go on vacation now; the toddler still isn't sleeping through the night.

- After I get the next promotion, I'm going to get better at work/life balance, I swear.

Some version of "When everything is settled, perfect, and locked in, that's when I'll finally do the thing."

Recognizing change as a constant is crucial for leading yourself; acceptance of change is strongly correlated to performance. More importantly, being able to operate in the face of change is imperative for your happiness.

No one should feel like they're constantly holding their breath, waiting for things to calm down.

The elusive certainty our brain so desperately craves isn't coming. Even CEOs get fired. No investment is guaranteed. You have no idea what the world has in store for you in the coming years.

71

Embrace Change and Uncertainty

You can let that be terrifying and sit on the edge of your seat for the rest of forever. Or you can accept it and feel empowered to control what you can right now.

REMEMBER

- IF YOU'RE ALWAYS WAITING FOR CHANGE TO BE "OVER" ... YOU'LL ALWAYS BE WAITING.

- THE ABILITY TO OPERATE IN THE FACE OF CHANGE AND UNCERTAINTY IS PARAMOUNT FOR KEEPING YOUR OWN SANITY AT WORK. IT ALSO MAKES YOU LOOK REALLY GOOD TO THE PEOPLE WHO ARE IN CHARGE.

- USING THE "THIS IS MY CHANCE" MENTAL PRACTICE ENABLES YOU TO REFRAME WHATEVER WAS THRUST UPON YOU (A CHANGE, AN URGENT ACTION ITEM, ETC.) INTO AN OPPORTUNITY. FOR EXAMPLE "AI IS SCARY, I WONDER IF IT WILL TAKE MY JOB" BECOMES "THIS IS MY CHANCE TO LEARN NEW TOOLS AND BRING MY UNIQUELY HUMAN SKILLS TO THE FORE."

- IT'S IMPOSSIBLE TO BE EFFICIENT WITH YOUR TIME IF YOU STICK WITH EVERYTHING YOU START. DON'T LET SUNK COSTS KEEP YOU FROM MAKING A CHANGE.

Part II

Behavior: Showing Up as Your Best Self
(Most of the Time)

In Part I, we focused on mindset: the thoughts and beliefs that fuel your career. Your thoughts direct your behavior, which forms your relationships. The loop keeps going, for better or for worse (see the following figure).

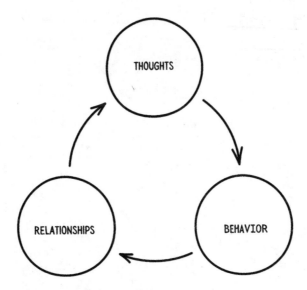

Leading yourself flywheel.

Negative thoughts and beliefs prompt suboptimal behavior and result in poor relationships. The inverse is true, too. Positive thoughts and beliefs prompt productive behaviors and result in strong relationships – most of the time, at least.

Leading yourself starts internally, then the internal becomes external. That's why I hope you read the first part. When you have the right mindsets, you've got a solid base, and it becomes easier to direct yourself to the different behavior (what you actually do) which then creates your relationships (how you work with other people).

This part (Part II) is about optimizing your behavior, and the third part is about strengthening your relationships. As you read these two parts, think about the mindsets you built earlier in the book: zooming in on your impact and the larger purpose of your work, losing your attachment to beliefs not serving you, overcoming your lizard brain, and making peace with uncertainty. These mindsets should be doing the heavy lifting at the start of the flywheel.

Chapter 5

Hit Goals with Momentum

"What you get by achieving your goals is not as important as what you become by achieving your goals."

—Zig Ziglar

D o you ever tell yourself you're going to go to the gym, and then don't do it? How about telling yourself you're going to finish all your reports by Friday, but then you let them sneak into your weekend? I'm certainly guilty of that one.

The problem with breaking promises to yourself is that over time, you learn that you can't rely on yourself. Your confidence shrinks, your work starts to suffer, and you become reluctant to lead, offer new ideas, or make bold moves.

This isn't a suggestion that you should start waking up at five to hit the gym, maximize every second of your work day, and never enjoy the human right of mindlessly scrolling your phone. You simply have to be sensible with your intentions.

> Most goals depend on consistency, not intensity.

The more realistic you can be with yourself, the more likely you are to fulfill your self-promises. The "I did it" momentum will push you to your next promise. To lead yourself, you must learn to balance aspirations with reality.

The Overpromising Trap

The vast majority of highly ambitious people have a common hang-up when it comes to goals: overpromising.

This shows up in one of three ways.

The Plate Spinner

It's not that you *can't* do each of the individual things you promised (proof the email, onboard the new hire, get the birthday cake, etc.), it's that you can't do them *all* at the same time. This is the hardest pattern to break because it's not a single promise that puts you over the edge. It's lots of little promises that at the moment seem totally doable, but collectively are overwhelming.

This often bites us when we make lots of little promises at work, then we make lots of little promises in our social life, and then we make lots of little promises to ourselves on top of that (like going to the gym, cooking dinner every night, and finally bringing the cat to the vet). The collective mental load makes your brain spiral and can eventually descend you into productivity paralysis, where you have lots of anxious energy and aren't even sure where to channel it anymore. A little stress everywhere adds up to a lot of stress. Keeping too many plates spinning is exhausting, and eventually impossible.

You might be familiar with David Sedaris's "Four Burner" theory. The concept is that your life is a stove with four major burners – your family, your friends, your work, and your health. The theory suggests that in order to be successful you have to cut off one of your burners. And in order to be *really* successful you have to cut off two (see Figure 5.1).[1]

So, if you want an awesome work trajectory and a thriving family, say goodbye to friends and fitness. If you want a social life and to be of optimal health, your family and work will suffer.

Personally, I think this theory is an oversimplification of how capable most people are of fluid prioritization. You can leave a burner on a simmer for a while. You can turn burners off and on through different seasons of your life.

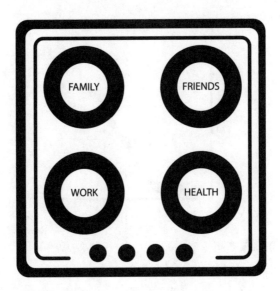

Figure 5.1 Four burner theory.

However, what the burner metaphor does correctly articulate is that you can't be performing at your absolute best in every single area of your life. There will always be a trade-off, which can be a nightmare for an overpromiser.

The first step for moving beyond plate spinning is to acknowledge that you can't, in fact, have it all. At least not at once. You have to make a choice, or the choice will be made for you, in the area you inevitably neglect. We'll dive more into when to phone it in in Chapter 7.

The Hockey Stick Projection

People who lead themselves are often inherently optimistic; it's part of what fuels them to take on big challenges. Yet, any virtue taken to an extreme is a vice. Setting too ambitious of a goal is likely to leave you defeated. In Silicon Valley, they call this the "hockey stick" projection. It's when a startup gives a presentation to a potential investor and the startup shows their revenue *slooowly* trending up. Yet, they are predicting a massive jump, just after the investment. The line of anticipated revenue looks like a hockey stick, like in Figure 5.2.

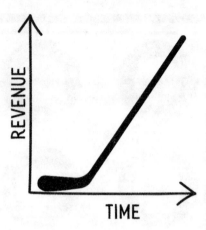

Figure 5.2   Hockey stick projection.

When you tell yourself (or worse, someone else) you'll do too much too fast, and you fall short, you feel terrible, even if you really did accomplish a lot. Overly ambitious goals, over time, erode your confidence.

Your self-promises should be optimistic, not delusional. You don't have to hit it every time, but you should at least be close.

One of my friends is a solopreneur. He sets a revenue goal for himself every year. He almost never hits it, but he always comes really close. And most of the time, he hits the goal the following year.

When achievement is within spitting distance, it's motivating. When it's nowhere near the realm of your current reality, your brain correctly ascertains that it should give up.

Learning to be intentional about setting ambitious yet attainable goals is how people go from being eager beaver self-starters (who eventually fizz out) to people who lead themselves and stay motivated over the long haul.

The "On Their Behalf" Promise

You can't control every element of everything. Making promises and setting goals that significantly depend on other people is not a good practice. For example, if you're an expert plumber, you'd never promise to build a house by the end of the year. That would be ridiculous. What if the carpenter falls through or the electrician makes some mistakes? What if the roofer doesn't show? There are too many variables.

It seems obvious in that example, but this phenomenon plays out in the corporate world all the time. Managers make promises, to themselves and their bosses, that depend on the work of their team. CEOs make promises to the board that depend on market forces and outside vendors. Perhaps you make promises to your own manager that assume so-and-so will send you the materials on time, another person will be available to weigh in on the draft, etc.

As you learn your organization more deeply, you'll become more accurate at gauging who you can count on for what. Yet, even with the most accurate predictions, it's best to set goals about your own behavior (the only thing you can control). You can't guarantee an overall output, but you can mostly guarantee what you put in.

> Shifting from output-based goals to input-based goals gives you a great sense of agency. You get more wins, and you experience yourself as more successful.

Here's how the shift from output to input might look in Figure 5.3.

Working backward from the ideal outcome to determining what you can, and can't, do to inform that outcome drastically improves the odds you'll meet your goal. This practice is crucial for your self-induced milestones and even more important when you're talking about goals with your manager. Making promises that depend on other people sets you up for an "it's so-and-so's fault!" if things don't pan out. Even if that's true, it's not a good look for you.

You've no doubt heard the Serenity Prayer: *God grant me the serenity to accept the things I cannot change, courage to change the things I can change, and wisdom to know the difference.*

I'm not religious, but I benefit from the reminder. Self-starters are often frustrated by their coworkers, or even their boss when it comes to missing deadlines or falling short in some way. The root of this frustration is usually

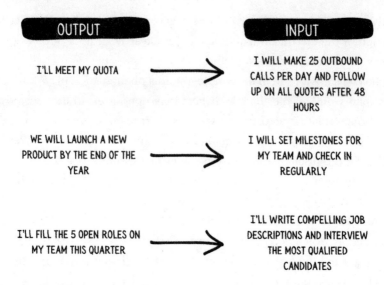

OUTPUT	INPUT
I'LL MEET MY QUOTA →	I WILL MAKE 25 OUTBOUND CALLS PER DAY AND FOLLOW UP ON ALL QUOTES AFTER 48 HOURS
WE WILL LAUNCH A NEW PRODUCT BY THE END OF THE YEAR →	I WILL SET MILESTONES FOR MY TEAM AND CHECK IN REGULARLY
I'LL FILL THE 5 OPEN ROLES ON MY TEAM THIS QUARTER →	I'LL WRITE COMPELLING JOB DESCRIPTIONS AND INTERVIEW THE MOST QUALIFIED CANDIDATES

Figure 5.3 Output to input goal shift.

because said self-starter made a promise, to themselves or someone else, that now *isn't* being fulfilled.

Thinking about what is and what isn't in your control can help you keep promises to yourself and others. On the flip side, overpromising and promising things that are outside of your control over time show the people around you that your promises aren't that meaningful. Even worse than that, you show *yourself* that your promises aren't that meaningful, thus, sabotaging your momentum.

Why Performance Reviews Result in Mediocre Goals

Humans have been judging each other since we were capable of comparative thought. Who is the best wildebeest hunter? Who never picks poisonous berries by accident?

Formal performance reviews, however, date back to roughly World War II, when the military started using metrics as grounds to dismiss poor performers. By the 1960s, General Electric and other big companies started to embrace performance reviews and give "developmental" feedback on a regular basis.

Today's performance reviews typically center around goals. What goals did you meet? What goals did you miss? And what goals do you have for the next pre-determined period of time before another performance review? Your organization might call these OKRs (objectives and key results) or some other acronym.

Managing performance is a best practice of ambitious people and organizations. High achievers don't want to be surrounded by people who aren't pulling their weight. Yet, the majority of performance reviews run into two challenges when it comes to goal setting.

Goals Default to Weaknesses

Performance reviews weren't initially conceptualized because everyone was doing great, so it's unsurprising that most reviews come with the dreaded *needs improvement* category. When your weaknesses are presented to you in a performance review capacity, the temptation, especially for high performers, is to make your goal: shore up said weakness. Yet, the research tells us the most motivating and achievable goals are built on your strengths.

Shoring up weaknesses that are sabotaging your performance and getting them to a point of "average" matters. Yet, over-indexing on weaknesses erodes your spirit. In one study, Gallup found that people feel more confident, self-aware, and productive when focusing on strengths rather than weaknesses.[2]

For example, if you never had an eye for detail, and you spend all of your time trying to train your brain to find typos, you're going to hate your life, and you'll probably still miss typos. The worst part is that you could've been coming up with new, innovative ideas in all that time you spent trying to train your unreceptive brain to see typos.

When you focus on your strengths, you enjoy your work more. You may lose track of time, unlock new levels of creative thinking, or experience more resilience. Enjoying the work and knowing the work is harnessing your skills breeds fulfillment. As a result, an organizational practice of strength-based goals leads to higher employee engagement, increased performance, and significantly lower attrition rates.[2] You're in charge of you; you'd probably like to be more engaged in your role and be an even stronger performer. It feels better than being bored and making mistakes.

We'll talk holistically about feedback (and what to do if it's not accurate) in Chapter 10. For now, my caution is this: Weaknesses are a data point to consider when you're setting goals, especially when you're setting goals in collaboration with your manager (like in a performance review). However, your weaknesses don't tell the entire story of your potential and shoring them up should not be the singular lens for your development.

Your professional goals should leverage what you're best at and should be (at least mostly) in alignment with your actual job description and what your organization has set out to achieve. Think about what your organization needs to accomplish in the next six months to two years. Consider your innate strengths. How can you push this forward in a way that's at least a little bit exciting to you?

Things like improving your intentionality as a leader, pushing to build relationships outside of your departments, or developing sustainable training for your team matter to the organization. Do they nicely ladder up to a key priority for this quarter? Not necessarily, but they do push the business forward.

Goals Are Directive

In addition to defaulting to weakness, goals are often only directed from the top. In many performance-based roles, your goals are handed to you, like meeting a quota, achieving a turnaround time, or hitting some other metric.

My hope is that your organization recognizes the benefits of collaborative goal setting, where in conjunction with your manager, you have a voice in the process of what your year is going to look like.

If that's not the case, you can layer on a (realistic) goal for yourself and share it with your manager. You might be thinking, *I just got this impossible number to hit, and now I'm supposed to add even more goals?*

Yes.

Why?

Because you might not be able to control the organization's output; you can control and be successful with your own input. The win for adding in your own goals is big:

- **Adding your own goals demonstrates to your manager that you're invested in growth, both yours and the organization's.** You're not nodding your head mindlessly, agreeing to all the strategic thinking other people did. Instead, you're owning your role, and giving thought to how you can harness your strengths to best serve the needs of the organization. Points for taking initiative and demonstrating leadership potential.

- **Further, adding in your own goals helps you feel more in control (because you are more in control).** Remember, self-agency is a cornerstone of leading yourself. Working toward a goal that you only partially control can be unnerving, especially if you don't have confidence in the people you're depending on. It's not very motivating and over time you can easily descend into one of those people who continually grouse about how hard it is to get anything done here. Extrapolating out what is within your control, what will make an impact, and what you're good at gives the anxiousness and ambition a place to land.

- **Most importantly, adding your own goal is a method of self-protection.** If a goal is handed to you from above, it's likely an output goal (like a revenue target). Remember, you're only in control of your *input*. Establishing a goal that focuses on your input, and sharing that goal with your manager, safeguards you against external variables.

  For example, if the edict from above is for you to make sure customer retention improves by the end of the year (outcome), your input may be to handle customer escalations within 24 hours, continuously elicit feedback from customers, and offer incentives to

83

customers on the brink of cancelation. You control what you can, but what if your organization has a major product failure resulting in huge customer churn? Now, you don't hit your decided-for-you metric. This is a recipe for an awkward performance review. But wait, 12 months ago your manager agreed that handling escalations, soliciting feedback, and offering incentives are paramount, and you did those things. The metric is still in the red, but your input is in the green.

Do you see how differently the conversation will go? This seemingly subtle difference is an example of how you can lead yourself within the existing framework of your job. You're not changing the output metrics, you're simply translating them into your own input behaviors.

When your manager agrees that a particular behavior or set of actions is crucial to achieving the output, and they see you doing what you talked about, less wrath and blame will fall on you if the number isn't ultimately achieved. This is playing corporate chess and using the protection of "not my fault" without seeming like a whiner. To be clear, it only works if it's accurate and you actually did the input.

Being handed a number can easily make you feel powerless, like you're just a cog in the machine and if you don't hit it, the year was a failure. Having something else to latch on to, even if no one is going to call you on it if you don't do it, gives your own year purpose beyond a metric.

As we go through the rest of the chapters on behavior in Part II, you'll continue to see how the mindsets you've learned in Part I (clarity of purpose, pointing your brain, quieting fear, and getting comfortable with uncertainty) enable you to avoid falling into the reactive behavior traps that plague so many disengaged, less than happy, underperformers. By leaning on your larger view, you are setting a different mental agenda for yourself, and following it with behaviors that are in alignment with that.

Good-Enough Goals (That Your Manager Will Approve Of)

Nothing gets me out of bed in the morning like a SMART goal . . . said no one, ever. You've likely heard of SMART goals (specific, measurable, achievable, relevant, and time-bound).

The SMART goal concept isn't bad in theory. A SMART goal is better than no goal or a vague goal. But if you limit yourself to SMART goals, you'll limit your thinking. SMART goals tend to be task-oriented. Like do the marketing report every week and do it exactly this way. With a sole focus on task completion, SMART goals have an important function, but they're rarely inspiring.

To lead yourself, you'll need to create goals that are bigger, longer-range, and typically more complex than simply checking off functional duties. Completing your tasks is table stakes.

It looks like a tall order. In reality, most goals won't check off all five factors. Some goals will be too ambitious, focus on shoring up a weakness, or be tactical, instead of strategic. That's OK; don't let perfection be the enemy of good.

Here's what we've covered so far. To effectively lead yourself, your goals should:

- Be mostly realistic (no over-promising here!)
- Focus on inputs in your control (instead of outputs out of your control)
- Play to your strengths (instead of over-indexing on resolving weaknesses)
- Align to your job and be in the service of the organization (because this place is paying you)
- Be intentionally and strategically crafted (instead of passed tasks from above)

Hit Goals with Momentum

Here are three examples of good enough goal-setting when you're leading yourself and still have a manager to report to:

- **Example 1: An inflexible manager with a hardline metric:** Suneetha works in sales. She has several metrics that she's evaluated on: closed business, profitability, customer retention, referrals, and more. Every quarter, she has a review with her manager, walking through the scorecard. During Q2, Suneetha's manager tells her that her customer retention metric is in the red. Many of her customers are ending their contracts after the initial trial period. Suneetha is frustrated. She knows the client onboarding process is clunky and customers face some significant technical integration challenges. Instead of getting defensive, Suneetha validates her manager. The customer retention metric is in the red; that's a problem. She then shifts the conversation to talk about: What are the inputs within Suneetha's control? How can she leverage her innate strengths of being a relationship builder? Suneetha agrees to proactively address customer retention, suggesting that she give each of her new clients a one-week check-in call to better understand the challenges they might be experiencing. In the conversation, she can solidify the relationship and get ahead of any major issues. The metric stands: Suneetha's manager still wants her to improve client retention. However, after this goal-setting conversation, Suneetha and her manager are aligned on what input from Suneetha will best impact that metric. No matter what happens with the customer retention metric, next quarter's review will be better (provided Suneetha actually makes the check-in calls).

- **Example 2: A well-intended but misinformed manager:** Caitlin is the manager of IT for a medium-sized business. She has three direct reports. Her boss, the Head of Operations, doesn't understand much about IT but has always been supportive of Caitlin and her ideas. Caitlin's boss comes to her with the suggestion that her goal this year should be to have a first-call-resolution (FCR) rate of 100%, meaning that whenever an employee has an IT issue, it's resolved with the first call, every single time. Caitlin knew this wasn't realistic. Some issues are complex and depend on the support of outside vendors. Caitlin shared with her boss that the industry standard for this metric was 70–80%. Her team was currently at 65%, so there's room for improvement, but not hugely. Caitlin also shared with her boss that the FCR rate was only one metric to consider. In fact, the team's FCR rate was low (compared to industry standards) because they had created a robust offering of tech-support guides the prior year. Employees only needed to call IT for major issues. Small things, like a password reset or a Zoom update, were now being resolved independently. Yet, ever the striver, Caitlin agreed that the FCR rate could still improve, but suggested 75% as a more realistic target. Caitlin's manager saw how well she understood the interplay between metrics. He agreed to the 75% and had confidence in Caitlin, even more than he would have if Caitlin just nodded her head and hoped for a miracle to hit a 100% FCR rate.

- **Example 3: A manager who jumps to conclusions:** Alex works in HR for an organization that is struggling to retain employees. During a performance review, Alex's manager expresses frustration around the amount of turnover. The manager tells Alex that they must be attracting the wrong people, proposing that one of Alex's yearly goals should be to find new recruiting avenues. Alex, who had conducted many of the exit interviews, had a different hypothesis. Employees said they were leaving because they didn't feel they had enough learning and development opportunities or any growth trajectory. Alex shared this hypothesis with their manager, and together they shifted the conversation to how they can lay out potential role trajectories in interviewing more clearly and offer more robust training throughout the year. The goal changed from exploring other recruiting avenues to developing a first-year training plan, aimed specifically at new hire development. The overarching desire to improve retention is still there, but Alex's path is different.

In each of those scenarios, the manager had a different level of fluidity in the goal-setting process. Suneetha's manager was inflexible, so Suneetha added some input-based goals that play to her strengths. Caitlin's manager was more collaborative in the goal-setting process, so she steered the goals toward a more realistic objective. Alex's manager was receptive to their input and together they created entirely new goals that were in the service of the organization and more strategic.

Suneetha, Caitlin, and Alex could have easily defined those goals *without* their manager. Through self-reflection and strategic thinking, they likely would have arrived at the same conclusion. When you're committed to leading yourself, there's a temptation to set goals in isolation.

In the introduction to this book, I said the people who are leading themselves have ordinary jobs, but their work experiences are anything but ordinary. They find more meaning, they experience more satisfaction, and they're higher rated by their manager and just about everyone else. The preceding three scenarios show why. In each instance, both the employee and the manager left the conversation with more clarity about the goals, and the managers walked away with a very positive impression of the employee.

By defining goals in conjunction with their manager, the goals carry more weight. When those goals are (hopefully) achieved, the success will play into their next performance review, future opportunities, and the relationship they have with their manager.

There is a risk in sharing your goals with your manager. The risk decreases when you don't overpromise and you don't promise things outside of your control, but it's still there.

There's also a huge upside. Your manager knowing the depth of your goal is likely to make you more accountable than a self-promise. It will also be more impactful, propelling the validation loop that you are a reliable and strategic person.

If (When) You Fall Short

Intentional goal setting reduces the likelihood of failure but it doesn't eliminate it. You will, at some point, fall short. It's a good thing. The University of Arizona released a study on the "85% rule" suggesting that if you never fail, you won't be challenged to continue and if you fail too frequently, you will be demotivated. The sweet spot for motivation and learning is an 85% success and 15% failure rate. Fail 15% of the time and you will keep coming back for more.[3]

It helps to remind ourselves that failure plays a role in any successful endeavor. Steve Jobs was fired from his own company, Oprah lost her anchor position covering local news, and after driving overnight through a snowstorm in 1961, the Beatles were told by huge music executives that they would never succeed. You can probably think of many less famous examples as well.

If you want a great reputation, and you want to be perceived as someone who is proactively leading themselves, how you handle failure is crucial. People who aren't leading themselves make excuses. People who rise in the face of failure consistently employ two seemingly conflicting core principles:

- **They own it (even if they aren't 100% responsible).** We see CEOs (the good ones anyway) apologizing on behalf of their teams all the time. Over the course of your career, you're probably going to have to do the same. When you fall short on a goal, it's tempting to want to pin the blame on someone else, a process, or a group. You want to preserve your reputation, and instinctively, you seek to avoid blame. Yet, even if the shortcoming is not entirely on you, owning your part makes you a more trustworthy and accountable teammate.

  When you say *I should have been more proactive* or *I didn't allocate enough time*, you're letting your boss know that you understand what went awry and they don't need to point it out for you. Good bosses want you to learn from your mistakes, so show them that you already have.

- **They don't jump to "I'm sorry."** In an effort to show we are owning our part of a shortcoming, many of us will err on the side of over-apologizing. Failure is a part of business and chances are, your boss has failed too. There will be times when you need to say you're sorry, but in a lot of cases, you're better off saying thank you.

If you set forth on an ambitious goal, and you somehow missed it (after you own your part), say to your boss: *thank you for giving me the chance to make this right*. This takes ownership, but it doesn't go into negativity or wallowing. It lets your manager know that you appreciate their support.

Unless you said something hurtful, intentionally sabotaged someone, or made some other moral lapse, you probably don't owe anyone an *I'm sorry*. You tried your best; it didn't pan out. Thank your manager for their support, understanding, more time, another chance, whatever they're willing to give you to move forward.

Side note: Saying "I'm sorry" to a toxic boss only proves them right. They're more likely to berate you when you continue to berate yourself. Stick with "Thank you for bringing that up" or "Thank you for your willingness to jump in on this." We'll talk more about toxic bosses in Chapter 8, but when it comes to missing a goal, don't feed into their (often disproportionate) reaction by over-apologizing.

If you're not failing at least some of the time, you're probably not trying very hard. Success is never linear; failure is part of the process. The more you can own it, face it, and move forward quickly, the more likely your "failure" will be a chapter in your story, not the ending.

The Magic Is in the Pursuit

What would you do if you won an Olympic medal?

I'm embarrassingly unathletic, so it's tough to imagine. I have to believe I'd at least hang it up, if not wear it to all my meetings, the grocery store, and maybe even to sleep. It's an insanely cool accomplishment, after all.

Apparently, that's not what actual Olympians do. Dr. Ruth Gotian, author of *The Success Factor*, studies the highest achievers, people like astronauts, Nobel Laureates, and Olympic champions.

The vast majority of Olympians she interviewed had their medal in a box, in a safe, or under their bed. Apolo Ohno, one of the most decorated Olympians of all time, had his medal in a brown paper bag in his sock drawer. Dr. Gotian was surprised and asked each Olympian why they didn't have their medals more prominently displayed. Winning a medal is the ultimate expression of achievement, right?

They all said some version of: *It was never about the medal.* As soon as their Olympic careers were over, they moved on to something else. The medal wasn't the ending point, just a part of the journey.[4]

Some less-world-renowned version of this has probably happened to you, too. If you've ever been vying for a new job, and finally get it, you often wake up the next day feeling . . . frighteningly the same. When you hit the metric, launch a new product, or finally turn in a manuscript, you feel incredible . . . until you don't.

It's like the twinge of anxiety at the end-of-the-year sales celebration. You're proud of yourself for making quota. Yet you're staring down an empty pipeline and an even more ambitious goal. From hero to zero, just like that.

In *All the Gold Stars: Reimagining Ambition and the Ways We Strive,* Rainesford Stauffer writes "With ambition, there is never a tidy 'after' or endpoint; it's generative because aspirations build on each other. There is never a single fulfilled moment because as we aspire, we expand. It makes fulfillment a process, a practice, not a grand finale. There is, as we know, always more."[5]

> Holding your breath until you meet the next goalpost, knowing that the post will move in a matter of days, sometimes hours after you meet it, is *exhausting*. The feeling of achievement is important but it's fleeting.

An essential element of leading yourself is recognizing what success looks like for you, taking a breath to enjoy the process, and taking pride in the fact that you're continually expanding.

Your life's to-do list is never done (until it's really *done-done*). Goals are crucial; they fuel momentum and give us something to latch onto in times of challenge. Yet, living your life constantly chasing them is a recipe for ultimate emptiness.

The magic will always be in the pursuit.

REMEMBER

- AMBITIOUS PEOPLE OFTEN FALL INTO THE TRAP OF OVER-PROMISING. THIS COULD LOOK LIKE PLATE-SPINNING (PROMISING TOO MUCH IN TOO MANY AREAS), MAKING A HOCKEY-STICK PROJECTION (PROMISING AN OVERLY OPTIMISTIC FUTURE), OR MAKING PROMISES THAT DEPEND ON OTHER PEOPLE. WHAT YOU PROMISE, AND THE GOALS YOU SET, DEFINE WHAT SUCCESS LOOKS LIKE. CHOOSE WISELY.

- YOU NEED TO SET GOALS FOR YOURSELF BECAUSE IT GIVES YOU SOMETHING TO WORK TOWARD, IT SHOWS YOUR MANAGER THAT YOU'RE INVESTED, AND IT SAFEGUARDS YOU AGAINST ALL THE EXTERNAL VARIABLES THAT COULD SABOTAGE THE ULTIMATE RESULTS.

- GOALS ARE CRUCIAL; THEY FUEL MOMENTUM AND GIVE US SOMETHING TO LATCH ONTO IN TIMES OF CHALLENGE. BUT ACHIEVING THEM CAN'T BE YOUR SOLE SOURCE OF IDENTITY.

Chapter 6

Don't Look for Energy – Create It

"Energy and persistence conquer all things."

—Benjamin Franklin

Have you ever looked at your to-do list and wanted to throw up? Or maybe you fight the urge to take a nap instead.

In a rapidly changing landscape, there's no shortage of projects, research, and deliverables. And there's never enough time. People who lead themselves are not immune to overwhelm, but they do know how to avoid emotional paralysis. By carefully managing their energy, they achieve more, with less burnout. To lead yourself, you'll need to make some calculated decisions about how to best leverage your brain power. It helps to know what gives you energy and what saps your energy. But remember you're leading yourself, not everyone else, so don't expect the world to shapeshift to your personal preferences.

Your Boss Doesn't Care About Your Enneagram

Honestly, I hate it when people ask about my Enneagram. I think I'm a 1, wing 8 or something? Whatever that means. (Enneagram lovers are probably like, "Of course, you're a 1!")

Enneagram is the current flavor of personality testing, but these types of assessments aren't new. For decades, researchers have been trying to categorize people into nice little boxes. Prior to Enneagram entering the workplace, Myers-Briggs was the big name. There's also DiSC, Clifton Strengths, Hogan, and tons of other versions of personality testing.

When viewed as a mere data point, personality tests can be helpful. Knowing your strengths, what you need in a relationship, how you get energy, and what's most likely to annoy you is generally beneficial information *for you*.

However, rigid personality assessment in the workplace typically presents (at least) one of three challenges:

- **People use their "type" as justification for poor behavior.** For example, when someone talks over people in meetings or acts on impulse, they're not "just being an ENFP" . . . they're being an asshole. And they can do better. This leads to challenge #2 . . .

- **People think they can't change.** Sure, we might have a natural inclination toward certain behaviors or be naturally gifted in certain areas, but those things change on their own over the course of our lives and they can change with intentional effort. These tests capture your brain at a specific moment in time.

- **People expect others to cater to them.** This one is the most egregious and self-sabotaging behavior and it can undermine your reputation in ways you're not even aware of. I want to make a distinction here; if you're in a marriage, knowing and appreciating each other's love languages brings you closer. Your extroverted friend who understands that introverted you needs some alone time when you travel together is a treasure. In deeper, more long-lasting, and important relationships, knowing and adapting to each other's types is a reasonable expectation. However, if your boss has 14 direct reports, they're not going to remember your Enneagram when doling out deliverables. Sorry.

If you want more self-knowledge and feel inclined to take the Enneagram test (or any other version), by all means, do it! Checking in with yourself and reflecting on your strengths or shortcomings is a valuable exercise.

Just don't let the "answer" limit your thinking or bind you to a particular way of working.

Truthfully, you're more complex and ever-evolving than your Ennea-gram suggests. No matter how many "wing types" you add.

Start Where It Feels Fun

To lead yourself, you'll need to balance the need to get high-priority things done with your own energy.

There are differing schools of thought on how to maximize productiv-ity and tackle your to-do list: Do you do the hardest thing first? What about three small things, to get a quick win? Should you finish the thing you started yesterday or jump to something new?

I follow the advice I got from Meryl Streep's husband (albeit indirectly). In an interview with Meryl Streep, a reporter asked her, "Where do you begin when you're learning a new character? The accent? The physical man-nerisms? The lines?"

She told the reporter that she'd adopted a simple philosophy she learned from her husband, who is a sculptor: start where it feels fun and easy.

If it's good enough for Meryl Streep, it's good enough for me, and prob-ably good enough for you, too. (Meryl and her sculptor husband are now separated, but the advice still stands.)

Start where you have the most energy to start.

When you're feeling down in the dumps, instead of looking at your to-do list based on strategic prioritization, start where it feels fun! The renewed mental energy you get from doing the fun part first enables you to get through the rest.

Starting where it feels fun is easy to understand intellectually. What Meryl Streep and her sculptor husband likely had working in their favor was big blocks of open time for their craft and the decision-making power to choose what part of it felt fun.

Assuming you're not an Oscar winner, it's unlikely that you were granted that level of space and authority when you showed up to work. You won't always be able to start where it feels fun. Sometimes the boring thing comes first because someone else who makes more money than you do said so.

However, you probably do have the space to make some choices about how you tackle things. More freedom naturally comes with time, but you can set the wheels in motion quickly with intentional behavior.

If you truly have no open space or flexibility, intentionally managing your energy is going to be very difficult. However, with *at least a little* autonomy can you actualize the practice of starting where it feels fun.

Even if you only manage to get 30 minutes a week to decide what you want to work on, use it on what you're most excited about. Your energy and enthusiasm will radiate to your less-thrilling to-dos. Here are a few ways to maximize the autonomy you have in managing your to-dos.

Block Your Sprints

In many organizations, calendars are visible. When you need to devote intense brain power and energy to something specific, make sure your calendar reflects that. Nothing will kill your enthusiasm like constant interruptions. Book a conference room, block the time, leverage the "do not disturb" tools at your disposal. Even if it's a sign on the back of your chair.

Confirm and Reconfirm the Prioritization

When you and your leader have clear timelines in place, your freedom to manage your own workflow will increase. The more clear you are at the start of a project or task, the less likely interruptions and false urgency are to show up later. We'll talk more in Chapter 8 about working for a boss who always changes their mind.

Create a Cadence

If you don't have a regular time for check-ins with your manager, this is your sign to set up a recurring meeting. The same is true for committees and project teams. When there's dedicated time to ask questions and get updates, people tend to save their pestering for the check-in, leaving you with more open calendar space to manage your work. Of course, things will come up, and these meetings will get pushed out or pulled forward sometimes. Remember, we're going for good, not perfect here.

Ask for Autonomy with Specificity

Autonomy means different things to different people. Perhaps for you, autonomy means the flexibility to decide when you're working on what throughout the month. Maybe for your boss, autonomy means they only check in with you at the start and end of the day. Clamoring for the elusive "more freedom" isn't likely to get you the calendar flexibility you're after. Be specific in how much control you'd like to have over your time and have a conversation with your boss about what is and isn't possible.

Politely Push Back on Interruptions

You teach people how to treat you and that includes your boss. Sometimes we're our own worst enemy, greeting disruptions with enthusiastic cheer. But if you want to lead yourself, you can be intentional about politely pushing back. With time, you can make inroads at how much autonomy you have and how free people feel to disturb your focus time.

First, validate the other person's intent. They want this to be successful (so do you). This could look like:

- I appreciate how invested you are in this project. I'm really excited about it, too!
- I know we all have a lot riding on this one!
- I'm eager to make progress on this!

Then choose a polite pushback:

- Can we go through the updates in more detail in our 1-1? I want to be sure I'm fully up to speed with the other parties and I don't have that intel on the fly.

- There are a lot of moving parts to this! Can you tell me what specifically you need to know?

- Would it be best if I proactively updated you on a daily/weekly/ monthly basis?

- Has the timeline we talked about regarding X changed? Just want to be sure I'm not holding you up!

The language here is kind and it's also clear. Through repeatedly using these talk tracks, many (self-aware) colleagues will get the hint that they're interrupting you for ambiguous "updates" or things that can wait.

Work from Where?

We can't tackle the challenge of leading yourself without discussing location. Your environment impacts your mindset, your behavior, and your relationships.

When millions of people transitioned into remote work in 2020, the bounds of "the office" were eroded indefinitely. Many found they were *more* productive without office distractions, commute time, and other interruptions. Others quickly concluded that focusing attention outside of the office environment was harder than anticipated. While some relished the absence of awkward small talk, others missed the camaraderie.

No matter which side of the spectrum you personally fell to, the vast majority of people became more attuned to *where* they do their best work. When lockdowns were lifted and options were more plentiful, there was an unsurprising almost universal request for more choice, autonomy, and flexibility, something big organizations traditionally don't respond well to.

Unsurprisingly, broad-sweeping edicts were issued, and companies typically landed in one of three camps:

- **You're going back, even if you're kicking and screaming:** "We have to return to the office for the culture!" touted senior leadership. That narrative often fell flat, especially when the culture in question consisted of fluorescent lighting, microaggressions, and uncomfortable pants. Most "return to office" plans fumbled big time. The majority of employees didn't react well to the notion that someone whom they'd never met and who had never done their job had determined where they'd be most effective. Oh, and it just so happens that it's the exact same place where those leaders believe everyone else will be most effective, too. This edict fueled the, in some cases accurate, belief that the prior year's narrative of work/life balance and flexibility was a well-timed facade.

- **Hybrid . . . but not like that:** Other organizations took a seemingly more flexible and collaborative approach. However well intended, this choose-your-daily-location approach led to a frustrating experience for both employees and employers. Teammates fought traffic only to sit on Zoom by themselves in a lonely office. Employers failed to capitalize on any perceived cultural advantages of in-office work because schedules were constantly misaligned. Some organizations tried to manage this by assigning "in-office" days or tracking badge swipes, ultimately erasing the cultural goodwill that comes with offering "flexibility."

- **Stay home, forever:** On the opposite end of return-to-office, some organizations cut ties with their office spaces, ending leases, investing in home-office materials, and putting a stake in the ground that work-from-anywhere would be a cultural advantage. For some, this was transformative in both productivity and quality of life. For others, it led to feelings of disconnection and insignificance.

There's too much nuance for one "right" approach. Wherever your organization landed, there's going to be an inevitable downside to it. Perhaps for you, the downside is quite significant.

You can change in one of two ways:

- Accept it. Make the conscious decision that your salary, the benefits, the industry opportunity, whatever it is, is worth the trade-off. Maybe

You may even be actively angry about the decision your organization made. If that's the case, and the policy is not going to change, you have to change. Otherwise, you're going to spend a lot of mental energy being angsty and waste a lot of time complaining. That serves no one.

you're only a couple of years away from a big pension (does that even exist anymore?). Maybe this job will set you up for the next big move and you just need to stick it out for a certain amount of time. Maybe this is your chance to build career-changing relationships. Own your choice and stop dwelling on what you wish could be.

● Find a new job. Seriously. If it's that important to you (and only you can make that decision), channel your energy from reactively complaining to proactively seeking a new opportunity. "But I can't!!!!" If you truly can't (which I find hard to believe), see above, Choice 1.

In the face of "return to office" mandates and continual re-definitions of what hybrid means, it's tempting to assume you no longer have control over your life. While it's true you may not get a say in what work environment your company lands on, what you are in control of is how you respond, and long-standing angst is never the right call.

Constant griping drains the energy of the people around you, and even more significantly than that, it drains your energy. You will eventually lose the ability to muster any type of enthusiasm, which is a terrible feeling.

Your energy needs are important; proactively working with your energy (instead of letting the circumstances drain it) has a major impact on your career. Having said that, where you personally feel in-flow is likely not the determining factor in where your organization decides work will be done. Still, you're not powerless. Let's talk about how you can thrive in less-than-ideal conditions.

Enduring Things (or People) Who Make You Tired

When you see it in your inbox, you audibly groan. You sink lower in your chair and the energy you had moments before vanishes. Maybe it's a project you hate working on, an office you hate working in, or even a person you hate working with.

To lead yourself, you must be able to temporarily endure things and people who make you tired.

If you know you're up against a mentally draining day (or longer), it's imperative to manage your energy in the ways you *can* control.

If you can't change what's in the center (task, location, person), change the peripheries.

The peripheries surrounding a drain could be the environment, who is in the room, what's happening before or after, and other micro-factors that can buoy your energy.

> Mentally succumbing to the idea the next however-long will be soul-sucking only ensures that it most certainly will be.

Here are 10 ways to improve your energy by modifying the periphery:

- Play music or a show you've seen before in the background. This is especially helpful virtually. Playing music before a virtual meeting, even if it's not everyone's favorite song ever, drastically changes the tone of the following conversation. It far exceeds the awkward, *let's give it another minute . . .*

- Drink a lot of water right beforehand. Being hydrated is energizing. You'll also get micro-breaks because you have to go pee so much, the short walks will give you even more energy.

- Have a walking meeting or a standup meeting. If cameras are the norm, turn them off. If camera-off is typical, go camera-on. An environmental disruption will give you a temporary jolt of energy.

101

- Wear your favorite outfit, or at least pants that don't dig when you sit. Personally, I work almost exclusively from home. I wear leggings most days, but they're leggings that I feel good in (and they're not the ones I slept in). Getting ready, whatever your version of that is, has an energetic impact.

- Schedule something you're looking forward to immediately following what you're not looking forward to. This little brain hack helps fend off waves of anticipatory dread. Yes, something not favorable is coming up, but so is something great! Maybe it's an exercise class, coffee with a friend, or a long shower.

- Start the conversation with something that isn't boring. Icebreakers can be awkward, but awkward and silly is better than boring. If you don't want to play two truths and a lie, open with a better question like "Tell me the most interesting thing you're working on this week?" or "What's something you're looking forward to this week?"

- Bring a favorite snack or beverage (ideally not edibles or alcohol). This sends a recurring signal to your brain that something positive is happening, albeit not necessarily the content of your task. You'll also have something in your mouth to slow you down before you say something you're not proud of.

- Invite a high-energy colleague to the meeting. Another person can change a bad dynamic quickly, without even being aware of it.

- Prioritize your sleep leading up to the drain. Going into something tiring when you're already depleted is setting yourself up for failure. If more hours of sleep aren't a possibility, focus on improving the quality of your sleep. Black out your room, turn on some white noise, and leave your phone facing down, so the blue flash doesn't disrupt your subconscious all night.

- Modify the lighting. For thousands of years, humans have learned to regulate our energy in reference to the sun. Natural light has a profound impact on our energy level. When the sun isn't available, well-designed LED bulbs can mimic natural lighting. Conventional fluorescent lighting is linked to reduced productivity and alertness. Why any office still uses it is beyond me. If you're working from home, pay attention to the color temperature of the light bulbs you buy. Some will make your house feel warm and cozy, others will make it feel like the hospital.

By adding peripheries or changing the circumstances of what would otherwise be draining, you're gifting yourself the opportunity for a more engaging or, at least, less soul-sucking experience.

While you can't always bring a fizzy drink or play your throwback jams, training your brain to look for ways to create a better experience for yourself gives you a sense of self-agency even before you act.

Sometimes your mindset will be the *only* thing you control. The good news is, it's the most powerful thing. More powerful than every element of the periphery. If you need a quick refresh on reframing annoyances into opportunities, flip back to the "This Is My Chance" practice in Chapter 4.

> This is the essence of leading yourself, looking around a seemingly fixed situation, and saying, *how can I claim my own sense of agency here?*

Give Your Brain the Learning Fuel It Craves

Have you ever watched a toddler master a new skill? Whether it's walking on their own or putting the pieces into a puzzle, the moment they get it, their whole body comes alive with delight. That's because learning something new creates a dopamine rush, which fuels your body with energy.

You're likely thinking, *I'm too busy with my job! I don't have time to learn.* In truth, you don't have time *not* to learn.

If you're not proactive about spearheading your own development now, you'll be forced to learn later (via layoff, industry change, corporate mandate, etc.). You've likely seen this play out with the person who refused to learn the new systems, clinging to the old software until they were forced to make a change. When they finally, grouchily adapted, everyone around them heaved a collective sigh of relief. Failure to keep learning is a hallmark of unsuccessful and consistently unhappy people.

Learning is rocket fuel for your career in the long term. It also has a major positive impact on your energy in the near term.

According to LinkedIn data, 94% of employees would stay at a company longer if it invested in their career. Yet the #1 reason employees feel held back from learning is because they don't have time.[1] High achievers don't wait for "perfect" conditions to learn. They squeeze it in, knowing an imperfect attempt is better than none at all.

It's obvious that learning propels your reputation and your energy, but learning is also the catalyst for more long-term meaning, joy, and opportunities. Here's how it plays out:

1. **Meaning:** When you know you're up to speed and actively integrating new learnings into your role, your confidence radiates. AI becomes a lot less scary when you know how to leverage it in your job. You begin to correctly see yourself more as a driver of your destiny.

2. **Joy:** Exposing yourself to new ideas and different perspectives gets you out of your personal (or organizational) rut. New experiences make us joyful when we come to them with openness.

3. **Opportunities:** Whether you want a better job, more flexibility, or the opportunity for a completely different career, learning propels the process. We are moving into a skills economy. No longer will where you went to school determine your destiny (thankfully). You have the power to make yourself more valuable simply by using the phone in your hand to learn something new.

You don't need to propel the quintessential quarter-life crisis of getting a graduate degree. Learning can and should happen within the bounds of your job. Learning in the flow of work peppers the meaning, joy, and opportunities that come from learning throughout your day.

You're likely already doing more learning than you're giving yourself credit for. The vast majority of us have learned over the last six months how to innovate, pivot our skills, and adapt to new conditions. The YouTube video you watched about the new software? The article you read about a competitor? The research you did on changing regulations? That stuff counts; it's naturally woven into the fabric of your day.

Taking on a stretch project can also give you a learning-induced energy burst. Jumping in to work on initiatives like onboarding, researching a new customer base, or developing sustainability practices enables you to learn while also producing something of value. Through the project, you'll be challenged to research, think deeply, and collaborate with people whom you may not ordinarily. Projects like this also make for a great "exceeds expectations" talking point for a performance review. Flip back to Chapter 3 for a refresher on when to raise your hand.

> Side note: Stretch projects also act as a forcing function, because when you volunteer to lead a project (unlike participating in a webinar), it's impossible to just skip it and lie to yourself that you'll listen to the recording later.

Instead of letting your emotional state depend on yearly events, like awards or potential promotions, prioritizing learning gives you a more regular dose of energy. Stretch projects, webinars, and figuring things out as you move through your job are all within your control.

Having said that, your organization is also likely offering you at least a few formal learning opportunities. I've facilitated a lot of these training sessions in the last decade on topics like Leading without Formal Authority, Purpose at Work, and of course, Leading Yourself.

When you think about training, pay careful attention to your energy. Are you excited? Or filled with dread?

Here's what I observe in the thousands of people my team and I have trained: The highest-performing people get the most out of training. They're also the ones who needed training the least. Why?

They come ready to learn. With a natural growth mindset, they volunteer, they ask questions, and they actively search for what they can take from a session. If the examples aren't perfectly aligned with the function of their job, they connect the dots and apply the principles to their own world. If the content is challenging at first, they push through instead of throwing their hands up. They recognize, *If I'm going to spend my time here, I'm going to make sure I get something out of it*. People who are leading themselves take the ownership of making their time count. Their determination is obvious, to me, to their boss, and to their peers.

Here's how that mindset shift shows up (see Figure 6.1).

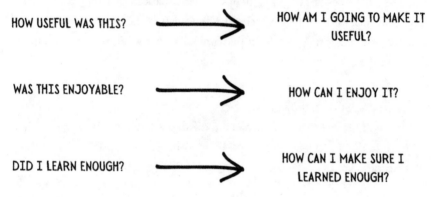

Figure 6.1 Learning mindset.

If you've made up your mind that training is stupid and there's nothing valuable you'll glean from it, you will prove yourself right. You will not get anything out of it. Alternatively, when you look for opportunities to learn, that's exactly what you'll find.

Ask any experienced trainer or facilitator, and they'll tell you less than 50% of training effectiveness is up to the leader of the training. Speaking from my own personal experience, I can run a program and have two different people in the room, both with the same job and the same boss. One will get nothing out of it, the other will have a transformative experience.

If you're not someone who is naturally predisposed to embrace learning, it might be worth thinking about your background to understand what might be behind your reluctance. One thing I say frequently to executives who are frustrated by their team's reluctance to engage is that *people don't come to you clean.*

Everyone enters training with a backstory about learning, and that backstory often determines how much energy they derive from learning something new.

If you're someone who did well in school and was praised by your teachers, maybe you show up ready to engage. But we're not all like that. Maybe you're the one who got chewed out by their former teachers for your unorganized backpack. Maybe you had an early-career boss who over-reacted to any mistake in the learning process, making you dread training sessions. Maybe you didn't do as well in school as your more compliant "school is fun" sibling did. Or maybe you grew up with parents who regarded training as something punitive; if you had to go, it meant you were a screw-up.

It could be anything.

It's typically not the fault of the organization or the individual leader when people don't embrace learning. But it's still a leadership problem to solve (and it takes more than a half-day workshop to rewire lifelong mental ruts). You can be part of helping that mindset change by being one of the people who show up eager to engage. You're not running the session but you're most certainly in the power seat.

Actively learning, especially in a group setting, is a vulnerable experience. Recognizing that you could do better, know more, or grow in some way is an act of courage, especially in a culture that rewards compliance and touts perfection.

Unfortunately, many fall into the false belief that learning is an energy drain. The risk of looking dumb in front of our peers, carving out the time to do a role-play or listen to the webinar, and opening an already-exploding brain to more information can feel scary and exhausting.

Yet, when you do it, even with those small learning-in-the-flow-of-work moments, your brain wakes up, and so do the people around you. You create a flywheel of growth, creativity, and fulfillment, which is a lot more exciting to wake up to than more of the same.

The choice is yours. You can create energy by optimizing your environment, harnessing your enthusiasm, and fueling your brain with learning experiences.

Or you can hope the fourth cup of coffee will actually do the trick.

REMEMBER

- IMPROVE YOUR STAMINA BY STARTING YOUR TASK WHERE IT FEELS FUN. THE RENEWED MENTAL ENERGY YOU GET FROM DOING THE FUN PART FIRST ENABLES YOU TO GET THROUGH THE REST.

- TO INCREASE YOUR CONTROL OVER YOUR TIME: BLOCK YOUR SPRINTS, CONFIRM PRIORITIZATION, CREATE A CHECK-IN CADENCE, ASK FOR AUTONOMY WITH SPECIFICITY, AND POLITELY PUSH BACK ON INTERRUPTIONS.

- IF YOU ARE BACK-TO-THE-OFFICE AGAINST YOUR WILL OR ARE SENTENCED TO WORK WITH PEOPLE WHO ARE DOWNRIGHT DRAINING, YOU CAN MAKE IT FEEL LESS SOUL-SUCKING BY MODIFYING THE PERIPHERY.

- WHEN YOU'RE LEARNING, YOUR BRAIN GETS ENERGY. YOU CREATE A FLYWHEEL OF GROWTH, CREATIVITY, AND FULFILLMENT, WHICH IS A LOT MORE EXCITING TO WAKE UP TO THAN MORE OF THE SAME.

Chapter 7

Know When to Phone It In

"The more you try to do, the less you actually accomplish"
—Chris McChesney, The 4 Disciplines of Execution: Achieving
Your Wildly Important Goals

Did you have an early career job you took *so* seriously? Most high-achieving adults have early career experiences they (in hindsight) viewed as disproportionately consequential.

For several years, I worked in a restaurant my then coworkers and I (not lovingly) referred to as Crapplebee's. I was a waitress, a hostess, a bartender, and even a kitchen expeditor. During the summer and school breaks, I'd stack double shifts, arriving at 10 a.m. and leaving at 2 a.m. It was great money, but it didn't come easy.

Anyone who has worked in a restaurant knows the exact type of chaos it comes with. Even the most high-end establishments have a "back of house" full of profanity and pandemonium.

I'm still not particularly good at being chill in lower-stakes situations, but in the early stages of being a working adult, I was truly terrible at it. Every derailment, mishap, or new corporate edict felt incredibly life-altering. Being out of chicken tortilla soup was a shift ruiner. The hostess triple-sat you when you're already in the weeds? I'm spiraling. During those days, I'd wake up in the night panicked that I forgot someone's ranch. To this day, I still remember every table number.

Looking back, I truly can't believe I cared that much. I was serving $1 Long Islands with what felt like the emotional weight of a neurosurgeon.

If I could go back and talk to my younger Crapplebee's self, I would tell her: it's not that serious.

You likely have countless memories of extending huge effort for something that didn't warrant it. You might even be doing it now.

The advice to "phone it in" is often met with great resistance from high achievers. Merriam-Webster defines phoning it in as "to do something with low enthusiasm or effort." It harkens back to the pre-Zoom world, originating from the notion of someone who can't be bothered to physically show up where and when they're expected. In today's vernacular, it's a decision to do the minimum.

Consciously deciding that you're not going to do your best is a tough decision to make. It can be challenging to not feel personally attacked by the suggestion. After all, being the slacker isn't *who you are*. But it's who you should play, at least sometimes.

If you try to be all things to all people all the time, you will fail. Either you choose when to phone it in, or the inevitable overwhelm makes a default choice for you. The problem with not proactively choosing is that you'll find yourself phoning it in with areas you would never have consciously decided upon (like your health or your family).

This chapter isn't a plea to get you to care less. It's a prescription to care more selectively.

I call this out specifically because interview after interview has revealed that being engaged, caring a lot, and working really hard to solve problems tends to be the resting state of a high achiever. But your biggest strength often winds up being your biggest weakness, too.

We all have more to do than we could possibly get done, and when you add in growth opportunities, the potential for overwhelm and burnout multiplies. Leading yourself requires that you be intentional and proactive about choosing to phone it in on low-impact areas.

Be Invaluable, Not Indispensable

We're often sold an early career narrative that hard work and perfection are the path to advancement. If you have any work experience to date, you've probably come to realize that this is not true. In fact, it's the opposite of true; overworking and striving for perfection puts you on a path to bitterness.

Occasionally and intentionally phoning it in is more likely to push you forward than it is to hold you back.

In part of my work as a consultant, I've been privy to many pre-promotion conversations. I've also been in many conversations that went the other way, discussing why someone wasn't getting the promotion, and how the leader was going to have to tell them. This gave me a unique insight into what leaders generally consider to be promotable qualities, and what disqualifies some people.

After paying acute attention to these conversations for several years, here are three common traps I see high-achieving, hard-working people fall into. These traps not only hold them back from advancement, but over time, they breed frustration and resentment.

- **Outworking everyone.** There will always be someone who is getting more done. If you've risen to the top by working through weekends, taking late-night meetings, and producing an exceptional volume of work, your pace is likely not sustainable. You'll need to find a new normal (if you ever want to sleep again). Take a note from Lee Iacocca, the leader who is widely credited with turning around Chrysler in the 1980s. He provides a perfect summary of this trap in his autobiography, where he writes:

  I'm constantly amazed by the number of people who can't seem to control their own schedules. Over the years I've had many executives come to me and say with pride: "Boy, last year I worked so hard that I didn't take any vacation." It's actually nothing to be proud of. I always feel like responding: "You dummy. You mean to tell me that you can take responsibility for an $80 million project and you can't plan two weeks out of the year to go off with your family and have some fun?"[1]

  Not everyone has the economic freedom or logistical advantages to take two weeks to be with family. And not everyone's CEO takes the same view on prioritizing family and self-leadership. While there's

Know When to Phone It In

some under-acknowledged privilege in that paragraph, the crux of the message is poignant. Overwork is not admirable, especially when it's at the expense of those you love.

People who lead themselves don't put themselves at the mercy of everyone else's schedule, and they don't consider overworking their superpower because they know that when you get to a certain level, overworking does more harm than good.

- **Being the only one who can do your job.** A couple of years ago, I was working with a customer success team at a financial services organization. There was one young man, Stephan, who was exceptional at troubleshooting technical integration challenges during client onboarding. Stephan's boss raved about him, always gushing about how fast he could resolve escalations and how he was the *only one on the team* who understood the backend of particular systems. Stephan had expressed a desire to move into a management role. When a role became available, he didn't get the promotion. Out of sheer practicality (or laziness), his boss decided Stephan would be too hard to replace in his current role. If you are the only one who can do something, that something is likely going to be your responsibility indefinitely. There's an ugly downside to being "irreplaceable."

- **Never making a mistake.** One reason high achievers overwork themselves is they're paralyzed by the idea of putting forth anything other than perfection. In Chapter 5, we looked at the research from the University of Arizona concluding that (some) failure can positively impact motivation.[2] Self-starters tend to think of failure as related to putting forth a really innovative idea and having it not work out. As you think about when to phone it in, consider that failure can be small, calculated choices too. You can let a deck go with typos or miss a deadline by a few days and still advance in your career.

If you're dying on the hill of believing that those three preceding attributes *will* in fact get you promoted (and you have some organizational evidence to prove that belief), fine. You might be right. Perhaps your organization does reward overworking, irreplaceable perfectionists.

However, I implore you to ask, *at what cost?* If the only way to get promoted is to sacrifice your entire life, be completely indispensable, and never make a mistake . . . is it a promotion worth having? Once you get it, will things change?

We'll talk more about making your next big move at the end of this book. For now, it's helpful to release yourself of the emotional pressure that overwork and perfection are the path to get where you want to go. Holding on to it will not help you prepare for your next play. It will only wear you out.

The research – and our experience – tells us that people who get promoted phone it in sometimes. They make calculated choices about what warrants big effort and what can settle for good enough. To lead yourself, you must bring your best self to the things that matter most. It can't be everything.

Choosing What Matters and What Doesn't

Now that we've aligned around the premise that you can't bring your best self to every single project or conversation, it's time to assess where to deploy your best efforts. People who are proactively leading themselves fine-tune their ability to pick out what matters most. They focus their efforts on getting the best ROI on their time.

To propel your career forward and keep your sanity in check, you'll need to weigh the long-term value against your personal level of daily joy. Here's why looking through both of the lenses is crucial for deciding what matters and what doesn't.

- **Why the long term:** You are the only one who is taking the long view on your life. No matter what your company's trajectory for your role suggests, you're in charge of your roadmap. It doesn't have to end with making Partner. Remember part of leading yourself is choosing your own destination. Flip back to the Introduction for examples of how different people have defined holistic success (for example, purpose, joy, promotions, money, creativity, freedom, reputation, etc.).

You don't need to have it 100% defined, but without some sort of intentional direction, landing ass-backward where you want to end up is unlikely.

As you assess your daily choices through a long-view lens, remember that sometimes the long term is really, *really* long. Way beyond a promotion or two. A new career path, a young child, or a startup will not reciprocate the level of intentional effort you pour into them for years if not decades down the road.

- **Why joy:** If you hate every second of the process, the odds of achieving any type of success are quite low. We've all seen the grin-and-bear-it person, white-knuckling it out until they can retire. Or worse, the parent so determined to be perfect, they wind up not enjoying a minute of the journey.

  Humans depend on joy and going without it consistently will prompt your creativity and strategic thinking to erode. Of course, you'll have to slog through it sometimes, but the goal is to not slog through it all the time.

Here's a quick and easy way to determine where to spend your time, and what to avoid. (Check out Figure 7.1.)

Let's walk through each category:

- **Long value and high joy:** Give it your all; this is the last place you should phone it in. Seems obvious, right? Easy to understand, more challenging to practice. Urgent to-dos often shift our attention away from this category, pointing our focus to the low-value, low-joy category.

- **Long value but not joyful:** Push through it; some degree of this is inevitable. No one's career is an end-to-end experience of glee, even if you work for yourself (some might say, especially when you work for yourself). Long-value, low-joy to-dos are typically things like learning a new system, creating sustainable processes, resolving recurring hang-ups, or teaching someone else how to do something. There's a win in the long term, though your energy might suffer in the

114

Leading Yourself

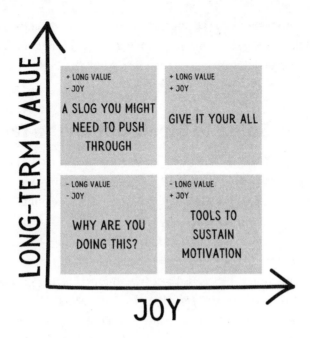

Figure 7.1 Choosing what matters.

near term. Flip back to Chapter 6 for strategies to sustain your energy through these long-term value must-dos.

- **Not valuable, but joyful:** Sustain your motivation with this category. If you're an ambitious person, it may be tempting to view these activities as a frivolous waste of time. That minimizes how important joy is. There's not going to be a solid line between everything you do and the success you achieve. Taking a break to listen to music or spend time with a friend often has a ripple effect on how you show up for (seemingly) higher-value tasks. Make the time to be present in these moments.

- **Not valuable, not joyful:** What's the point? This category will fill you with dread. Though sadly, it's not entirely avoidable, particularly if your assignment has been doled out by a corporate overlord. For most of us, there will be times in our careers that are just plain draining. These are the places where you phone it in. You do just enough to get by, saving your brainpower and energy for things that matter more. (Note: if your entire job is falling into this category, it might be worth reevaluating.)

Nobody Is Going to Bleed Out on the Table

Several years ago, I was working with an international bank in deep turmoil. They had an unsustainable amount of defaulting loans, they were in trouble with government regulators, their internal systems were failing, and several people on the executive team actively hated each other. The dashboard was bleeding red and the energy in the room was suffocating.

Nobody wanted to own the current situation, and everyone had a different idea of how to best proceed. Voices were raised as the executive team wrestled with how to move forward. As the conversation escalated, some executives started to stand up, slam their notebooks closed, and take the conversation to a level of personal insults.

The head of HR, whose sister worked in an Emergency Room, snapped, shouting over the chaos, "Let's get a grip. Nobody is going to bleed out on the table!"

It was a grounding reminder in a moment when people were definitely lacking perspective. Yes, it was a high-stakes situation, but the reality was, no one was going to die. That comment didn't solve the problems, but it brought the group headspace to a place where solving problems was even a possibility.

Now, to be clear, this wasn't a Crapplebee's out-of-chicken-tortilla-soup situation. This was serious; hundreds of jobs and hundreds of millions of dollars are high stakes. Yet, still, nobody was going to bleed out on the table.

If you're working in an ER, I'm sorry . . . this doesn't apply to you. The "nobody is going to bleed out on the table" is a mantra used to put corporate problems in perspective. I often find myself repeating that phrase when things go wrong.

The fact that the HR leader's sister was an ER nurse gave her a deeper perspective. No matter what happened with the regulators or what system was failing, it wasn't life or death. Because of her personal (albeit second-hand) experience with actual life and death issues, she could approach

116

Leading Yourself

serious workplace issues with less anxiety, which of course enables you to see things more clearly and solve problems more quickly.

But not everyone spends their weekend listening to their sister's tales of bleed-outs in the ER. For the rest of us, it's easy to lose perspective and assume that the challenges in front of us are life-altering crises.

Three factors tend to exacerbate a lack of perspective in the corporate world:

- **You're not doing much of anything else.** It's not surprising Crapplebee's felt so serious. It was all I was doing for 16 hours a day, every day. If your hobbies, friendships, and personal time have vanished, the environment is ripe for taking work too seriously.

- **Other people also lack perspective and you hype each other up about it, creating a loop of even less perspective.** We feed off of each other's emotions (more on that in Chapter 11). If everyone around you is radiating manufactured crisis vibes, your brain will pick up on the subtle cues of unrest and join the "party."

- **There's not currently a crisis somewhere else in your life.** High achievers love the rush of problem-solving. Their brain needs something to latch onto, so much so that they'll sometimes, even subconsciously, create a crisis. At work, this behavior can be rewarded. I hope you never face a significant personal crisis, but if you do, you'll be surprised how insignificant work problems become.

Next time you feel like you're pouring from an empty cup, banging your head against the wall to solve unsolvable problems, or bending over backward to please a boss who won't notice, ask yourself: Who is going to bleed out on the table if you don't?

Beyond Your 9 to 5

At risk of eliminating my consulting business, I'll say something most executives probably don't want their people to hear: sometimes you should 100% phone it in at work. Not just on a particular project or initiative; I'm talking about phoning in your whole job. Not forever, but temporarily.

117

Whether it's due to a life stage, illness, or perhaps because this isn't the right job for you, sometimes doing the minimum is a fine choice.

When I first came back to work from maternity leave, I told my husband that I thought my brain was broken. I couldn't remember anything. In hindsight, some of that was definitely sleep deprivation. But some of it was that I was allocating so much of my "learning and remembering" capacity to something not work; I was learning how to be a mother. I pored over articles about starting solids, I read books about baby sleep, and I took infant CPR courses. The list goes on. In the first few months of motherhood, my brain and body were working overdrive on my new 5 to 9 (or, uh, 5 to 3 a.m.). Because of that, I missed a few deadlines and phoned it in a few times at work. I made that choice semi-consciously. In hindsight, I wish I had been more intentional about it.

At first, I was reluctant to include this example. I didn't want to come clean about it, because I didn't want to feed the myth that mothers are too distracted to work. But then I realized it was only for a short time, and it wasn't about being a new mother, it was about being a new parent, which is something that's going to happen to much of the workforce.

Perhaps you have something going on in your life that is consuming your brain. There are times when you can decide that your 9 to 5 is not as important as your 5 to 9. It might be for a week, it might be for a month, it might be for longer. It doesn't make you a bad person. It doesn't even make you a bad employee.

You could choose to make a reprioritization because:

- **You're over-indexing on your side hustle.** One of my friends is an aspiring filmmaker. He's pouring every ounce of his heart and soul into his indie film. From 9 to 5, he works as a lighting guy in a corporate studio. He's not passionate about it, it's simply an economic necessity. He does a decent enough job at work and preserves his energy for what matters most to him.

- **You're in a different season of life.** Having a new baby, caring for an ill parent, or navigating a health challenge yourself will take more from you than your after-work life did in previous seasons. To fully attend to what matters most right now (child, parent, your own health), you will simply have less to give at work.

- **You're not experiencing any reciprocity.** If you're pouring your all into your job, you deserve to get something back. This could be a strong feeling of purpose, a great salary, or even being appreciated. If the "give" is a never-ending one-way street, you may choose to stop giving so much. Don't make this choice in active anger; daily resentment is an exhausting experience. You can decide to phone it in, but if you do it with a "because you don't deserve my effort" chip on your shoulder, you'll pay more of an emotional price than your organization will. This phone-it-in is a temporary move until you find better.

Accepting a shift in focus instead of berating yourself over a personal failure can be challenging, especially if work-related success is (or was) a key pillar in your identity.

In *All the Gold Stars: Reimaging Ambition and the Ways We Strive*, Rainesford Stauffer reflects on her own pandemic experience, saying, "I received two calls simultaneously during the first few weeks of March 2020: one was from my dad, telling me he'd taken my mom – who he thought was having a heart attack but actually had COVID – to the emergency room, only to be turned away and told to come back when she fully couldn't breathe, when her lips were blue. The other was from my manager at my then part-time job I felt lucky to have hung on to that long, wondering why I was a minute late to a Zoom meeting if I was truly at home 'doing nothing.'"[3]

There's nothing like a boss demanding minutia while you're facing a personal crisis to help you clarify your priorities. During the pandemic, many people made the conscious decision to stop being the world's best employee. Spurred by side hustles, life changes, and a lack of reciprocity, "good enough" became the new bar, especially in working remotely.

This shift showed up in some pretty creative ways:

- **People hire assistants to do their jobs.** Every job has elements that are tedious and don't require full brain power. With tools like

Fiverr a few clicks away, some teammates outsourced the easy or boring parts of their job, making the choice that a little bit of expense was worth the amount of time they got back.

- **People take on two jobs.** During the pandemic, some had the realization they could do OK-enough at two jobs with the same amount of effort it took to be great at one job. Instead of getting one salary and a modest performance bonus, they got two salaries and no performance bonus. In a world where a living wage is increasingly difficult to find, it's unrealistic to think innovators won't find a workaround.

- **People use AI to work drastically less.** Even in creative and strategic work, AI is useful. ChatGPT, Bard, or other AI tools might not produce an exceptional work product . . . but with the right prompt, they can give you a running start. It's typically easier to edit or modify something "average" than it is to create "excellent" on a blank page. Sometimes the robots are, in fact, good enough.

Now, many companies have wised up, and have clauses in their employer agreements that limit outsourcing, using AI, or actively working for competitors. If your company has no such clauses and this has given you a few ideas on how you, too, can phone it in, then so be it.

Overcoming the Mental Hurdle

The conscious choice to phone it in at work is one of the most challenging decision points for people who are leading themselves. When your career is built on giving it your all, not prioritizing your job feels scary.

Very few people have the luxury of rewriting their entire career in the face of new personal priorities. You likely have bills to pay and a future to think about. Yet, consciously deciding where you'll invest your mental horsepower, and where you'll phone it in enables you to be at peace with a less-than-perfect performance at work. It's a decision you own, not one you fell into.

When it comes to phoning it in, there are many gradations: from the top performer gunning for a promotion who phones it in on the least strategic aspects of their job, to someone nursing a dying parent who's decided being present is more important right now, to the aspiring filmmaker showing up for his day job while saving his creative energy for his passion, to the unappreciated employee doing just enough to hold on to to their paycheck while they search for something better.

Your review is unlikely to note the times you were present for your family, took care of your health, or fed your soul with an outside-of-work project. Your tombstone will not read "exceeds expectations" or "delivered a valuable return to shareholders." In 20 years, the only people who will remember if you worked late all the time will be your family.

> Wherever you fall on the striving scale, it's important to remember your performance review is not your life review.

Work can and should be a source of purpose, fulfillment, growth, and joy. Loving your job is an amazing feeling; doing work that you know matters contributes to a meaningful life.

But it's not your whole life. In some seasons, it may only be a small piece.

You are the one in charge of you. When you're leading yourself, you proactively decide: What and when will I phone it in?

REMEMBER

- LEADING YOURSELF REQUIRES THAT YOU BE INTENTIONAL AND PROACTIVE ABOUT CHOOSING TO PHONE IT IN ON LOW-IMPACT AREAS.

- YOU WILL NOT GET WHERE YOU WANT TO GO (IN THE LONG TERM) BY OUTWORKING EVERYONE, BEING THE ONLY ONE WHO CAN DO YOUR JOB, OR NEVER MAKING A MISTAKE.

- FOCUS YOUR EFFORTS ON TASKS THAT HAVE LONG-TERM VALUE AND A HIGH LEVEL OF JOY. TASKS THAT ARE JOYFUL (BUT DON'T OFFER LONG-TERM VALUE) ARE STILL USEFUL TO SUSTAIN YOUR MOTIVATION.

- IN THE MOMENT, IT'S TEMPTING TO VIEW WORK-RELATED PROBLEMS AS MORE CONSEQUENTIAL THAN THEY ARE. REMIND YOURSELF, THAT NOBODY IS GOING TO BLEED OUT ON THE TABLE.

Part III

Working with Other People (Even Annoying Ones)

In Part I, we grounded ourselves in the core mental abilities for lead-ing yourself mindsets (identifying purpose, looking for the best, quieting fear, and embracing uncertainty). In Part II, we talked about translating that mindset into behavior – from setting the right goals for yourself to managing your energy and knowing when to phone it in.

Now it's time to tackle the area of the workplace that gives us the most problems: other people. And there's no relationship that bumps up against our desire to lead ourselves more than the one we have with our boss.

Let's walk through how you can apply leading yourself to *improve* your relationship with your boss and your colleagues, even through times of awkwardness or stress. I'll also cover how you can lead yourself even if you disagree with a decision your organization makes and how to apply self-leadership to finding your next play.

Chapter 8

Boss Management

"Having a bad boss isn't your fault. Staying with one is."

—Nora Denzel

Your manager might be an awesome, emotionally intelligent, expert prioritizer who always makes time to support you . . .

Or they might not be.

Even if they are pretty good most of the time, they won't be every single day. Because just like the rest of us, your manager is a human. They, too, get stretched thin, fight waves of burnout, and have a less-than-perfect boss they're trying to please. It's unlikely that you'll ever know the full extent of the pressure your manager is under, personally or professionally.

There's a great scene in the movie *The American President* that captures this dynamic. The president (played by Michael Douglas) is anxious about a brewing fight with his political rival. Over a game of pool, he explores the options (none of which are good) with his chief of staff AJ (played by Martin Sheen). Should the president ignore his rival baiting him in public? Should he make a threat behind closed doors? Or should he risk his reputation and fight fire with fire in a public forum? His chief of staff passionately urges the president to take the fight public.

The president snaps back, "Is the view pretty good from the cheap seat AJ?," frustrated by impassioned advice from someone who wasn't going to face the challenge of implementing or the consequences of a wrong decision. Whatever advice he took or didn't take, the president was the one who would have to go out and sell it to the world, and ultimately, it was he who would pay the public price if it didn't work. His staff may have been well intended, but they weren't sitting in the hot seat; they had the sideline view from the cheap seats.

The cheap seat quagmire plays out every day in the regular working world. The people in the cheap seats often have the benefit of after-the-fact knowledge; that's why they're so confident in their opinions of what should have been done by the people who had to act before that knowledge was available. When you're in the cheap seats, you don't have to understand the full context, nor is there any risk of taking action that would put you under the microscope.

> It's easy to know what needs to be done when you aren't the one who will have to do it. You can more easily see what needs to be said when you aren't the one who will need to say it.

Phrases like "armchair quarterback" and "voice from the peanut gallery" capture this challenge, too. Even if your boss is a jerk who keeps pushing back your 1-1, the truth is, you don't know what it's like to be them. In this instance, you may be the one in the cheap seat.

When I was in eighth grade, I was on my middle school's dance line. At the start of the season, we voted for a team captain. We elected a girl who was an incredible dancer; she was in private lessons, had been in commercials, and was cast to perform in *High School Musical* at a fancy theater in Atlanta. Because of all these commitments, she missed practice a lot. The rest of us were frustrated; she was in a leadership role, but hardly ever showing up. In venting to my mom, one of my friends said, "You'd think she'd know better than to commit to too many things at once; she's in eighth grade!"

My mom howled with laughter and it took me several years to understand why. Now, it's obvious, of course, an eighth grader isn't an expert prioritizer and obviously she's going to miss practice with our crappy dance line to go to an audition with a talent scout. At the time, I overestimated the ability of a 14-year-old because of her leadership role as team captain.

Surely I (who was a terrible dancer by the way) would know exactly how to juggle all of these demands if I were in her position.

You should have high expectations of your boss. They're also human. They take on too much, and say the wrong thing, sometimes. Just like you. Don't assume they have it all figured out because they're one step above you in the org chart.

High performers recognize that the, albeit imperfect, relationship you have with your boss is one of the most important factors in career growth.

Leading yourself isn't a sentence to operating alone on an island far removed from the directives, guidance, and opinions of your boss. Self-leaders work in collaboration with their bosses. They play to their boss's strengths, make the most of sometimes limited 1-1s, and through their own intentionality, form better relationships with their boss.

Your Boss Is Not Your Servant (and You Aren't Theirs, Either)

When Robert Greenleaf coined the phrase "servant leadership" in a seminal 1970 essay, it was a much-needed improvement over the traditional command-and-control leadership model that had prevailed for centuries.

According to Greenleaf, "The servant-leader is servant first. It begins with the natural feeling that one wants to serve. Then conscious choice brings one to aspire to lead. That person is sharply different from one who is leader first, perhaps because of the need to assuage an unusual power drive or to acquire material possessions."[1]

Servant leadership was a crucial stepping-stone into a more humane world of work. But the world of work has changed a lot since the 1970s. When Greenleaf originally introduced servant leadership, a typical manager likely supervised a small functional team. They didn't have their own deliverables, they weren't on multiple cross-functional initiatives, and they didn't start their day answering an onslaught of overnight emails.

Today, as middle management continues to thin out, leaders typically have between 11 and 15 direct reports and their own high-stakes deliverables.[2] These exhausted managers often justifiably feel they don't have the time to devote to servitude.

More than 50% of managers are feeling burnt out.[3] If you're not burned out yourself, you could very likely be working for someone who is. When leaders are tired, overworked, and stressed, serving can feel like pouring from an empty cup.

The current corporate fixation on "leader as servant" has become so intense, it's making people not want to be managers at all. *Time* magazine's viral piece "The Worst Year of Your Career Begins When You Become a Boss" rang true for millions. Further, a survey from Visier, a workplace analytics software company, found that less than half of millennials and Gen Zers aspire to be a manager.[4]

Let's look at the other side of servant leadership. Having a boss serve you sounds great on the surface, but in reality, the dynamic of being "the served" probably isn't doing you any favors.

When you lead yourself, you don't wait for a boss to make you happy or organize your work. Nor are you dependent on your boss's good favor to find meaningful projects or set your daily to-do list. When you're leading yourself, you know you can set goals, come up with new ideas, and get things done without waiting for your boss to serve up perfect conditions. This increases your own sense of agency, and candidly, is more likely to improve your relationship with your boss than someone who sits around expecting their boss to be the perfect servant leader.

> The most effective boss-employee relationships have evolved to be a collaborative partnership, with both parties working in tandem toward a shared purpose.

I recognize that servant leadership has been an altruistic, sacred ideal for a few decades now. But the model is rooted in a one-up one-down hierarchy that doesn't reflect the way the world actually works anymore. You've likely seen your own organization become less hierarchical. Today's org charts often resemble a jungle gym more than they do a ladder. Leading without formal authority is on the rise and begs the question: Who is the servant and who is served?

When you strip away the peripheries of your roles and the assumptions behind power dynamics, you and your boss are likely working toward the same thing. See the distinction in Figure 8.1.

COMMAND AND CONTROL LEADERSHIP

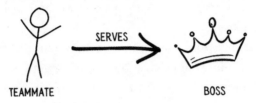

SERVANT LEADERSHIP

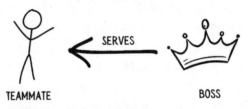

PURPOSE-DRIVEN LEADERSHIP

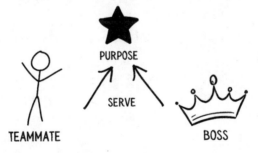

Figure 8.1 Purpose-driven leadership.

When leaders and teammates alike are in the shared pursuit of a cause bigger than themselves (their team, their customers, their community) and their goal is to positively impact their constituents (versus simply serving them), everyone winds up with more meaning, joy, and opportunity.

Ideally, your boss (and organization) will be clear about that purpose and why it matters. If they're not, you can take the reins as a self-starter by asking questions to clarify the ultimate goal.

Purpose-driven leadership is more complex than the cut-and-dried flows of power offered by command and control leadership or servant leadership. It's also more effective and true to the collaborative spirit of high-performing teams.

Making the shift from servant leadership to purpose-driven leadership benefits both you and your boss. And most importantly, as someone proactively leading yourself, you don't have to wait for your boss. You can start the process simply by aligning your conversations to support your organization's purpose and high-level goals.

Yes, your boss will likely have a stronger voice in charting the course and they'll probably keep veto power. Still, the "who is serving who" dynamic is more like a fluid dance than an eternal edict. You both have different strengths, different workloads, and contribute to the purpose of your organization in unique ways.

A shared purpose is also an imperative for goodwill. It helps you and your boss see that you are likely two people trying their best to accomplish the thing you agreed on, even if you go about it in ways that are sometimes annoying to each other.

The more you align with your boss on a purpose, the less "who is serving who" will matter.

Servant leadership brought us to a more compassionate, human-centered work environment. Yet, in today's environment, it's a narrative that's not helping anyone. Your boss doesn't want to be your servant and you probably don't want to be theirs either. You both want to do work that matters and support each other along the way.

Beyond Status Updates: Making Your 1-1 Impactful

Done well, 1-1 meetings can have a major impact on your work product, career trajectory, and overall happiness at work. Yet too often, 1-1 conversations are rushed, overly focused on deliverables-du-jour, or at worst, get postponed until there is "more space in the calendar."

Have any of these ever happened to you?

- Your boss cancels your 1-1 at the last minute after you spent time preparing.

- You wish your boss would cancel your 1-1 at the last minute because you have too much to do, you're not prepared, and your 1-1s generally aren't valuable.

- You and your boss agree that there's urgent business to tend to, delaying your 1-1 so many times that you eventually decide to skip it.

It's a frustrating experience. Fortunately, it takes only one of you to change the dynamic. Let's start with making sure you have the opportunity to transform these obligatory blocks of updates into something that moves your career forward.

For a 1-1 to be impactful, it has to actually happen. We're all busy, and the odds of your calendar magically one day freeing itself are quite low. Because 1-1s aren't typically viewed as urgent, they're easy to kick down the road. Resist this trap.

Continually delaying these longer-term, developmentally focused conversations can be costly in the long run. After a few rounds of "next week, I promise!" your strategic thinking, engagement, and morale will start to fade. You will pay a steeper price than your manager for not having standing 1-1s. They likely have multiple directs, their own boss, and a lot going on. If you're performing well, there's (seemingly) very little for your boss to lose by delaying or canceling a 1-1 with you.

You, on the other hand, will miss out on guidance, opportunities, and the chance to develop a good relationship

> Without these grounding conversations, both sides of the relationship can become untethered, descending into an overloaded inbox of status updates.

Boss Management

with one of the most important people in your career. I often think about 1-1s like exercising. Will missing a workout kill you? No. Will continuing to de-prioritize your health in favor of more "urgent" tasks cost you in the long run? Absolutely.

Taking the time to ground the work and the relationship always pays off. If your 1-1 is repeatedly being canceled or pushed back, don't reply with a fronting "no problem!" or "all good!" because it is in fact a problem and it's not all good.

An effective 1-1 tends to hit three buckets:

- **Near term.** What are your current projects, are they on track, and what resources do you need? These are the immediate must-dos. It's easy for a 1-1 to end here (don't let it).

- **Long term.** Think about and discuss the trajectory of your industry, the purpose of your organization, and your unique skills. Where do you see opportunities to try something new or get out ahead of a potential threat? Your 1-1 is a great time to talk about things that you don't typically find time to discuss in the cadence of daily business.

- **Personal growth.** Your manager is likely a kind person who wants the best for you. Having said that, they're probably not lying awake at night thinking about what you'll be doing three jobs from now. Use your 1-1 to ask about growth opportunities inside your organization, like playing a support role on a particular project. You can also look to your manager for advice on how you can be more effective in your role or pick their brain on what they think you should be learning. Imagine your manager's response if you asked them, "What are the top two things I should be working on learning right now?" Your manager may not bring these things up, but most managers are very receptive when asked.

All three elements are important; you may not hit each one every time, but you want to be consistently addressing all of them (see Figure 8.2).

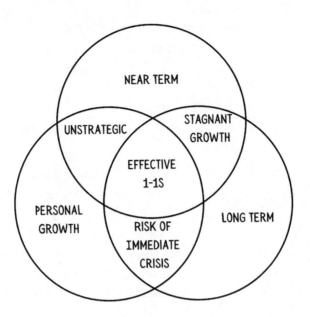

NEAR TERM

STAGNANT GROWTH

UNSTRATEGIC

EFFECTIVE 1-1S

PERSONAL GROWTH

LONG TERM

RISK OF IMMEDIATE CRISIS

Figure 8.2 1-1 Priorities.

Your tone and conversation don't need to be rigid; you can stay loose while (generally) following the structure. A more subtle win for having a standard flow for your 1-1s is it makes it harder for your manager to de-prioritize it. A casual "let's get together and go through things" is easy to punt. A structured conversation with a clear agenda is more difficult to wiggle out of.

You only own half of this conversation (maybe less, if your boss is an over-talker). Yet, making the most of your part can drastically alter the course of your 1-1. Just because you're not doing most of the talking doesn't prevent you from proactively guiding things.

Here are five things you can do to improve the effectiveness (with no help from your boss).

- **Prepare.** When meetings are back-to-back, it's easy to come Dukes-of-Hazzard style skidding on one wheel into this important conversation. Take a few minutes before the conversation to think about what you'd like to accomplish in terms of delivering updates, mitigating challenges, and discussing longer-term topics.

- **Address the near term first.** This is likely the pop-up window in your manager's brain. It will be easier for them to lean into longer-term topics and career development if they know none of your immediate deliverables are on fire. The more prepared you are to discuss the status of your work, the faster that part of the conversation will move, and the more time you will have for longer-term discussions, like your career growth.

- **Take notes.** This makes coming prepared much more feasible. When you can confidently start the conversation with "Last week we talked about XYZ and the update on that is _____," the pace of the meeting is more efficient. Taking notes also enables you to look for themes. In conversation, themes are easy to miss. For example, you might only spend one minute of the hour discussing a particular roadblock. In writing, they become more obvious. You're more likely to notice the things that make the list every week.

- **Ask questions.** You want to get the most out of your boss. Hopefully, they have more to offer than nodding along in agreement as you rattle off your updates. Questions are the jump-start of robust discussion; otherwise, your 1-1 is just a report-out. Ask questions about your boss's biggest priorities, what feedback they have on your work, and how they see you growing in the future. You should not be talking 100% of the time and you shouldn't be merely responding to *their* questions.

- **Confirm that you are meeting your boss's expectations.** This is pure self-protection. You may think you're opening up the door to criticism. . . . You are. It's better you hear it now when there's time to do something about it than being blindsided in a performance review months later. Ideally, your boss would bring this up without you asking. But sometimes they don't. They might not even realize there's something you should be doing differently until asked directly: *Is my work output meeting your expectations?*

1-1s don't have to be haphazard conversations about the crisis-de-jour. You can take the reins in these conversations to make them balanced, strategic, and meaningful.

Surviving Your Boss's (Annoying) Idiosyncrasies

Even if you have a great boss, at some point, they'll annoy you. Don't worry, you'll inevitably annoy them at some point, too! It's part of any long-term working relationship and it magnifies when you both care about the work, which, hopefully, you do.

An ideal leader has a high level of clarity around what needs to be done and why. They also don't want (or can't have) a high level of control and granular involvement in how it happens. They give significant autonomy and decision-making power to the people who work for them. These leaders aren't without fault, but they generally create more high-trust, high-performing teams.

If you have a leader who does this 75% of the time, consider yourself lucky.

Boss challenges tend to arise when they're trying to exert too much control, or they haven't provided enough clarity.

Take a look at Figure 8.3 and see if any of these jump out at you as a description of your boss.

Again, your boss is a flawed human just like the rest of us, with their own problems and pressures. None of these categories make your boss a bad person; it's simply a description of how even good bosses fall into some pretty common traps.

As you read these, think about how your boss communicates and how they make decisions to identify which category they lean toward. Following the descriptions, you'll find suggestions for how to work effectively with this type of leader.

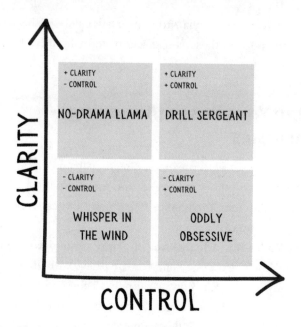

Figure 8.3 Clarity and control boss challenges.

The No-Drama Llama: High Clarity, Low Control

Often the most desirable leader to work for, this boss sets a clear and compelling vision and then gets out of the way. This "shout when ya need me!" approach to leadership can be helpful, provided you can and will remember to "shout!" However, sometimes, having this No-Drama Llama boss early in your career or immediately after joining a new organization can leave you feeling undersupported. It's not likely that your manager is intentionally undersupporting you. More often, this is your boss giving you a high level of autonomy because they trust and respect you. This boss typically responds best to:

- **Direct requests to help on something specific.** Asking for their help or support builds a stronger connection with your boss, and also helps you learn. But it's not a make-work task, like when you ask a toddler for "help" unloading the dishwasher. Really think about what your manager is good at. Maybe it's brainstorming, building relationships, or having a detail-oriented lens on things. How can you leverage their best thinking or most useful experience?

- **Being given time to think.** No-Drama Llamas are typically more strategic leaders than the other three alternatives. They're often very intentional in what they say because they believe what they say should be clear and concise. If you need this boss's help, give them a heads up in advance and always give them time to consider something fully before expecting an answer.

- **Clarification between directives and advice.** This boss wants you to feel a high level of autonomy. Because of that, they'll likely phrase what they need you to do as a suggestion or advice (when really, it's a directive). Like, "It would be great if we could dig into that in more detail." You can fend off future awkward moments here by clarifying whether or not their wise words are truly a suggestion to consider or something you're expected to act on.

- **Transparency.** This boss is giving you a high level of trust and in return, it's your responsibility to be candid if things aren't going well. Do not mistake a lack of request for "updates" to mean that your boss doesn't deserve to be informed, especially when something goes wrong that will affect the organization.

Whisper in the Wind: Low Clarity, Low Control

Working for a whisper-in-the-wind boss can be a very frustrating experience. What do they want? You don't know! When do they want it? No idea! How should you go about it? Couldn't tell ya! This boss might be disengaged, burned out, or going through a personal time when work simply isn't a priority. They could also just be an unintentional, absent-minded leader. You'll never know, so better to give the benefit of the doubt and work with what ya got, at least for now. This boss responds best to:

- **Urgency building.** This isn't a suggestion to manufacture false urgency for the sake of finally getting a response to your email.

What you should do is accurately paint the consequences of something going unaddressed: you miss an opportunity, a customer suffers, the team will be left in a lurch, whatever it is. This boss (unfortunately) may need an incentive to engage.

- **Brevity.** If you need help with something, get to the point quickly. Whether they're disengaged or just too busy, their attention span will rapidly deteriorate when faced with a high volume of details.

- **Stacking your questions.** If your boss is hard to get ahold of, save up your questions or requests so you can tackle multiple things in one conversation. This prevents you from spending a disproportionate amount of time tracking them down. Or sending more emails for them to ignore.

Drill Sergeants: High Clarity, High Control

This boss knows exactly what they want, how they want it done, and will follow up with you every few hours until it's completed. They were definitely a safety patrol in school, always wanted to be the line leader, and did their share of tattle-taling. These leaders often have a strong sense of right and wrong and can be a bit of a perfectionist. This boss responds best to:

- **A regular check-in cadence.** Is your manager constantly blowing up your phone? Having a designated time to check in can help fend off unwarranted interruptions. Even if this check-in is more frequent than you'd like (for example, daily), a standing meeting gives your manager a place to land. When they know they're talking to you soon, they're more likely to save their questions and comments. Quiet your manager's (sometimes irrational) fear that things are out of control by proactively keeping them in the loop.

- **Articulating the cost of micromanaging.** Most of the time, micromanagers don't realize how much time and energy they're costing you. And let's be honest: you usually answer their call with a "Hey, of course I have time!" . . . right? Respectfully establishing the cost of bottlenecking, constant updates, or check-ins can help your manager see things more clearly. You can say something like, "I appreciate how involved you'd like to be with this! Just a heads up; sometimes the status updates interrupt my workflow. Could we set a regular time to check in? That way, we can both be efficient with our time." Stay factual and respectful, but don't shy away from transparently communicating just how much time and energy you're spending.

- **Boundaries.** You teach people how to treat you, and that includes your manager. Yes, you need to respect their preferences and abide by the hierarchical norms of your organization. But the more you take after-hours calls or continually jump through hoops to loop them in, the more that behavior becomes the norm. Establishing boundaries early sets the tone for a productive relationship, where neither party becomes resentful.

Oddly Obsessive: Low Clarity, High Control

This boss will nitpick a typo in an email, but not realize the entire strategic plan is destined for disaster. They're easily influenced by whoever talked to them last, what other organizations are doing, or the TikTok they saw this morning. An oddly obsessive boss will constantly change their mind, not consider the context of their decisions, and will give after-the-fact directives that would've been helpful to know way earlier. Unfortunately, they tend to lose the engagement of their team quickly because no one knows what to expect and no one has the autonomy to do their job. This boss responds best to:

- **A tee-up.** Before you present something for them to respond to, lay the groundwork. Proactively explain the context of the project, why it matters, who is involved, and what the expectations were (because they definitely forgot). Bring your boss's full attention into the conversation by setting the stage for them to engage effectively. Without this tee-up, they will not consider the context of their directives.

- **A defined weigh-in period.** Their obsessive energy needs somewhere to land, and when you make a space for it, it's less likely to sneak up on you in the final hour. Ask for this boss's input early in the process and put some parameters on when the idea/feedback/edit phase is over. An oddly obsessive boss will struggle to let things move forward because each time they come back to it, something new is jumping out at them. Give them a defined amount of time and clear deadlines to keep things on track.

- **Polite pushback.** Sometimes these bosses don't realize the amount of rework or confusion they leave in their wake. They make decisions quickly, often based on feelings or a perceived sense of urgency. You can ensure they really mean what they say by politely pushing back with questions. You can ask questions like: What impact do you envision that having on our team's goals? If we resolve that, what do you think will change? What will happen if we re-prioritize that? Tone is everything; be genuinely curious. For all you know, they've deeply thought about those things already. If they have, the answer will be obvious. More often, though, these questions prompt an oddly obsessive boss to walk their words back and reconsider.

They're (Probably) Not Doing It On Purpose

A boss may bounce between all of these styles over the course of a year. Stress levels, their personal life, and even how much sleep they got the previous night can make an impact on how they show up for you and your team.

It's highly unlikely your manager woke up this morning and said to themselves, "How can I make sure my employee feels no support, autonomy, or empowerment?" They had their own series of events, be it working for a micromanager themselves or trying to lead a team who consistently let them down, that brought them here.

These idiosyncrasies can be frustrating because they can impact how you feel about work, how you perform at work, and often, what happens (or doesn't happen) for you beyond this job. Yet, these are all normal human grievances, bound to pop up in your boss, their boss, the people who work with you, and the people who may work for you. The better you're able to proactively manage them, the less consequential they'll be. When you make the decision to intentionally lead up, most bosses can become the cheer-leader, door-opener, and growth-creator you want them to be.

Most . . .

How to *Temporarily* Work for an Asshole

I started this chapter with the suggestion that your boss is (likely) an imper-fect human who makes mistakes sometimes. There are exceptions. Some bosses are assholes. They're mean, manipulative, and condescending. And you shouldn't have to work with them.

If while reading about your boss's humanity and likely good intent, you found yourself mentally screaming "But not my boss!," see if this list applies:

- Your boss intentionally makes you feel small, stupid, or underserving of opportunities.
- Most people inside your organization do not have a positive relation-ship with your boss.
- They use phrases like "tough love" or "it got me this far" to defend mean behavior.
- Your boss frequently complains to you about their boss, your cowork-ers, or your organization (even in an attempt to foster connection).
- Your boss has a history of bouncing between jobs quickly. It's always someone else's fault when it doesn't work out.
- Their personal life is somehow constantly in shambles (years on end).
- They've ignored your requests of them for things like more coaching, clearer feedback, standing 1-1s, or other reasonable managerial asks.

If you're consistently checking off more than a couple of these, your boss is probably in the asshole category. Perhaps they had a difficult childhood or they might be in the midst of a personal crisis, but that doesn't excuse their behavior, and it sucks you're paying the price. I'm truly sorry. So, now that we've acknowledged this injustice, what do you do? The obvious answer is: get yourself a new job.

Not always a viable option, for typically a few reasons:

- **Money.** Few people have the economic freedom to up and leave a toxic boss with nothing else lined up. A move takes planning.

- **Career growth.** Maybe this is the opportunity of a lifetime and your resume really needs the boost to get to the next threshold.

- **Other factors outweigh this frustration.** The coworkers you love, the generous PTO, the money, and other perks can be a powerful (albeit temporary) Band-Aid for working for someone insufferable.

- **You think you can stick it out.** Maybe this is a new boss, just after a re-org, or a temporary situation (like your amazing boss being out on parental leave). If the end is in sight, you may be tempted to grin and bear it.

> Emotions are contagious, and the longer you work for an asshole, the more likely you are to become one.

The preceding are all viable reasons for not leaving your toxic boss *tomorrow* . . . but they're not sound reasoning for the long term. Working for a toxic boss takes a toll on your spirit, your reputation, your work performance, and even on your outside relationships and health. If you're making it work for one of these reasons, set a firm time limit of one year or less. Oftentimes when people leave toxic situations, they find the "irreplaceable" money, perk, growth opportunity, whatever they were attached to, is actually quite replaceable. You won't know unless you look.

I know you don't think you'll become an asshole too, but you will if you wait long enough, and you won't realize it until it's too late.

Here are four strategies self-starters have used to (temporarily) deal with a toxic boss.

Repeat Their Expectations Back to Them and Get It in Writing

Using phrases like "to confirm, the plan is XYZ" or "based on this conversation, I'm going to ABC" with a toxic boss shrinks the room for interpretation. Clear expectations are a gift to both parties. Some toxic bosses speak without thinking, and only when you repeat it back to them do they realize they actually didn't mean what they said. For important things, get those same expectations in writing, even if it's you sending a recap email after the conversation. Paper trails are power. If your boss is constantly changing their mind, forgetting what they said, or giving you poor directions, having it in writing is key to protecting yourself. *Hopefully* you never need it . . . beyond an "attaching your initial email for reference!"

Use "You-Told-Me" Statements

This is kind of like truthful, professional gaslighting. It's a little bit manipulative but it's incredibly effective if your boss previously said something they are now contradicting (common in poor leaders). A toxic boss is reluctant to disagree with themselves. Rarely will you hear an "I misspoke" or "I shouldn't have said that." They usually just drop it, even if they grumble.

Consider this example: your boss tells you there's an onslaught of customer issues thanks to a bug on your website. Cue crisis mode (easily activated in jerk bosses). They're blowing up your phone, "We have to fix this issue ASAP!!! Drop everything!"

So, you send an email confirming that you will fix it ASAP. The next week, your boss asks about the status of the rebrand initiatives. You're behind because you spent a lot of time on customer escalations. They're pissed, because *obviously* you don't see the importance of the rebrand, and you *clearly* lack time management. Duh. Here's a you-told-me to reverse the dynamic:

> On Friday you told me rectifying these customer escalations was the top priority. I personally reached out to # of customers and the resolution was Y. Attaching the recap from our Friday conversation confirming the reprioritization, for reference!

Flipping debates back on them weakens their power, even more dramatically if you have the receipt to prove it. It's generally not a best practice to be defensive and manipulative with your boss, but if you're up against a jerk, it might be all ya got.

Stop Leaks

If you go home to your spouse and spend an hour venting about how awful your boss is, congratulations, your asshole boss now owns nine hours of your day instead of eight. Once you've decided to stick it out for three months, six months, a year, whatever it is, you have to put guardrails around the plague, or the rest of your life will start to become infected.

Guardrails might look like:

- I'm going to vent about my boss for 20 minutes every Friday on the way home and then be done with it.
- I'm going to go for a run to calm down after my 1-1 every week.
- I'm going to write down all the things I hate about my boss and then close my notebook until I quit.
- I'm going to scream into my pillow as loud as possible immediately when I get home and then I'll move on with my evening (don't knock it till you try it).

The more you mentally rehearse and unpack their awfulness and the more you bring it into your other relationships, the more power you give them. That's the last thing your toxic boss deserves.

Add a Buffer

Your career growth, learning, and opportunity do not need to stop because you're working for a jerk. If your boss is falling short (or actively working against you), build up your support system outside of that relationship. This could be through a mentor, a professional development group, going to a conference, or even taking an online course. Take the initiative to fill in the gaps your boss is leaving on their desk. A bad boss can temporarily steal your sanity; don't let them steal your future, too.

Making the Most of an OK-Enough Boss

Unfortunately, "failures" in leadership are typically a slow agonizing grind, riddled with hurt feelings and missed opportunities. If your boss isn't living up to your expectations, you're not alone. Most people have or will work for a less-than-stellar leader at some point in their career.

Yes, your boss plays an important role in your job trajectory, but you're still in the driver's seat of your career. It's up to you to identify your boss's strengths, calibrate to a shared purpose, and build a relationship that serves both of you. It's also up to you to create the emotional and practical guardrails you need to do your best work.

Remember, your career is about leading yourself in the direction you want to go, not constantly reacting to a less-than-ideal boss.

REMEMBER

- CALIBRATING TO A SHARED PURPOSE CAN HELP YOU AND YOUR BOSS COLLABORATE, PRIORITIZE, AND WORK TOGETHER MORE EFFECTIVELY.

- 1-1S ARE VITAL, EVEN IF YOUR BOSS ISN'T GREAT. THEY'RE ALSO EASY TO SKIP OR POSTPONE. DON'T MAKE THAT MISTAKE. REGULARLY MEET WITH YOUR BOSS TO DISCUSS NEAR-TERM GOALS, LONG-TERM GOALS, AND YOUR PERSONAL GROWTH.

- WHEN YOU PROACTIVELY MANAGE YOUR BOSS'S IDIOSYNCRASIES, THE LESS CONSEQUENTIAL THEY BECOME.

- WORKING FOR AN ASSHOLE IS NOT ACCEPTABLE IN THE LONG TERM. IN THE NEAR TERM, USING STRATEGIES LIKE "YOU TOLD ME" AND REPEATING THEIR EXPECTATIONS BACK TO THEM CAN SAVE YOU SOME HEADACHES.

Chapter 9

Disagree and Commit

"Honest disagreement is often a good sign of progress."

—Mahatma Gandhi

Leading yourself doesn't mean that you're unilaterally in charge of everything. Quite the opposite; leading yourself is about harnessing the power you do have, even if there are some things out of your control. There will be times (maybe frequently) when your boss, department leader, or CEO makes a decision that you disagree with.

You may be the one who is right, but from a career satisfaction perspective, that generally doesn't matter. In a recent McKinsey survey, only 57% of respondents agreed that their organizations consistently make high-quality decisions – just slightly likelier than a coin toss.[1]

The ability to move forward with a plan you're not entirely in agreement with is a hallmark of a high performer and good teammate. It's also imperative for not going insane in the corporate world, where you will inevitably disagree with many decisions your organization makes. The "I told you so" moment is never as sweet as you think it will be.

Trust the Experts

When I was in high school, my mom was the president of our church. Our church was small, humble, and at the time, quite visually dated. The walls were dark, dinged, and stained. In a push to attract new members, a portion of the modest budget was allocated to paint the sanctuary.

This was a Unitarian church that was, almost to a fault, inclusive of any and all opinions (if ya know, ya know).

Naturally, the congregational assumption was that everyone would vote on what color the sanctuary should be. My mom, with decades of experience leading people, knew that a church-wide vote would be a grievous mistake. Nobody was going to be voting. Instead, she appointed a team of three people – one member who was an interior designer, another member who was an architect, and the head of the children's program – to make the decision as a small group.

It was a very smart leadership move on my mom's part. Why? Let's say there was a church-wide vote. Here's what would likely play out:

- A portion of the members are happy; their color choice "won." They *clearly* have great taste.

- Another portion are annoyed, stewing every Sunday about how ugly the winning color is.

- Another portion are resentful, their color choice didn't even make the ballot!

The church was painted yellow and that was that. Was everyone thrilled? Probably not. But the decision had been made by people with expertise, so the congregation quickly moved on.

> If you work for an organization of any size, there are going to be decisions made that you disagree with. These might even be decisions you have to live with every day, even though you never got a say in how they were decided.

You might not believe the people behind your organization's decision-making to be as qualified as a designer, an architect, and a Sunday school teacher were in choosing a church paint color. I won't argue with you there; I've never met your executive team.

But I do hope that you see why not everything can be a vote. Not only is it inefficient, but it also often results in more hurt feelings and tends to over-index on the loudest voices rather than the most knowledgeable.

In instances where you find yourself frustrated, I invite you to humbly consider the possibility that there might be something you don't know. Even decisions that make your job harder could be the best call for your organization.

For example, in early conversations, some church members thought the church should be painted white. It's nice, bright, and airy. The head of the children's program knew that toddler hands would ruin that in a matter of minutes.

Another portion of the group thought the church should be painted blue; it's calming. The architect knew that because the church was north-facing, it didn't get enough natural light. Blue would feel cold and sterile.

Another portion thought the church should be painted red; it's lively. The designer knew that red wouldn't be conducive to reflection or tranquility. It's too stimulating in a big space.

At the time, I would've voted to paint the church white. I love a clean aesthetic. Five years ago, when I was the decision-maker, I painted the interior of my entire house white. Now that I have my own sticky-handed toddler, I can confirm white was a bad option. Good thing I wasn't in charge of painting the church.

When you're unhappy with a decision, it could be that others have more expertise, and you don't see the whole picture. It could be that it's better for another important part of the org, even though it makes your part harder. Or it could be that it's a bad decision because the leaders don't have the depth of understanding that you do. Whatever the case, leading yourself means that you have to navigate the space between rolling over and agreeing to everything and being a stubborn fuss who always demands things go their way.

Disagree and Commit in Action

"Disagree and commit" is a way to navigate that nuance. It's a model that requires you to speak up and also support leadership when the time comes to move forward. One organization that embraces this mentality exceptionally well is LinkedIn. LinkedIn has the reputation of being an innovative, fast-moving brand. They're also huge, employing almost 20,000 people with corporate offices spanning 30 locations. In a hyper-competitive environment, quick decision-making is imperative. For a large organization, that can be challenging.

I've worked with LinkedIn in different capacities for several years, as an instructor, a consultant, a speaker, and a workshop leader. I've seen them adapt as the environment and their business changes. As their offerings have grown (LinkedIn Learning, Recruiter, Ad Sales, etc.), their team has had to evolve in their approach to the market.

On a recent consulting engagement, our team worked with David Cohen, the former VP of North America for LinkedIn. After a restructuring, his new senior team was coming together. Their challenge was to quickly figure out how they'd work effectively to reach some very ambitious goals.

In a conversation about team values, David used the phraseology "disagree and commit."

The disagree and commit practice originates from Amazon. Here's how Amazon describes it:

> Leaders are obligated to respectfully challenge decisions when they disagree, even when doing so is uncomfortable or exhausting. Leaders have conviction and are tenacious. They do not compromise for the sake of social cohesion. Once a decision is determined, they commit wholly.[2]

I was surprised when David suggested it, especially to a relatively new team. I was even more surprised to see his team nodding along, everyone agreeing that "disagree and commit" would become an important pillar of their team dynamic.

I asked David more about why he chose this language in one of our 1-1 conversations. Here's what he said:

> It has become more commonplace for companies to want to be collaborative (lots of good reasons why). The challenge with collaboration is that people have transposed collaboration with consensus

building. Those are not the same thing . . . We got into this challenge at LinkedIn. I felt like our business – the talent solutions business – was falling prey to consensus-driven outcomes.

The way "disagree and commit" was deployed on my team was at the end of the day, I as the leader of the team may make a decision that was unpopular. I might make that decision because I have a different perspective on things, I might make it because we have different resource constraints now than when we first started thinking about this idea, it may be because of the broader LinkedIn context. I will hear all arguments and opinions. I want us to confront an issue and beat it up. But at the end of the day, I'm asking each person that as a member of the team, if you believe I've heard and understand your argument, and I still make a decision you disagree with, you commit to the direction that we're going.

This gave them permission to actively voice concerns, knowing that in the end, they would all be expected to commit to the decision that was made. The "disagree" part wasn't about trying to draw lines in the sand or igniting combativeness. It was passionate discourse from people who cared.

In the ensuing years, David's team lived by that value. Once the decision was made, it was made. No one sat in the background starving and sulking waiting to be proven right. They committed fully, even to things that weren't their first choice. The disagree and commit model builds trust and respect, for everyone.

After many months of implementation, David reflected on the principle, saying, "It had great results. It made decision-making faster. It made people

> We've all seen instances where someone disagrees and then doesn't commit, hoping that once the decision fails everyone will see that they were right all along. But holding your breath to be proven right certainly doesn't serve your organization, and more importantly, it doesn't serve *you*.

Disagree and Commit

feel more comfortable disagreeing and objecting to whatever the consensus seemed to be. It's allowed everyone to have a voice. It also helps people not take it personally when things don't go their way."

It's important to note: David was willing to hear out all arguments and explain his decision-making when people had questions. Your leader might not be as intentional, but you can still implement "disagree and commit" when you're leading yourself, even if it does nothing more than quiet your own angst.

Lingering in disagreement keeps you emotionally on guard and reluctant to lean in. Ultimately, you'll either be:

- Wrong, and have wasted a lot of mental energy and invested a lot of emotion digging your heels into the sand.

- Right . . . now what? Your organization made a bad call, is in a tough spot, and everyone is remorseful. Do you think you're going to get a personal apology from the CEO? Probably not. And even if you do get recognized for being right, saying "I told you so!" to people you at least partially care about doesn't feel good.

In many cases, you'll never even know whether the decision you wanted would have been better than what was chosen. Most business decisions don't fall neatly into a cut-and-dried category of "amazing" or "terrible." The majority are somewhere in the murky middle, and there are often unexpected consequences no matter what path you choose.

You're better off stating your recommendations in the deciding phase, and then committing to support your team when it's time to implement, whether you would have chosen that direction or not.

Appeasing the Illusive Corporate Overlords

Have you been victim to a corporate mandate, change, or goal that was obviously concocted by someone with no understanding of your job? Their lack of contextual understanding makes you want to scream, "That's not how it works!"

It's like when your elderly relative tells you to apply for a new job by walking in with your resume and a firm handshake, or when an Instagram finance expert suggests cutting out coffee to combat an impossible housing market and crippling inflation.

When someone makes a suggestion for how things could improve, without fully understanding how things are, it can be difficult to see any merit in the suggestion. Nowhere is this more pronounced than in a performance review.

As organizations become increasingly wide (versus tall) and specializations start to narrow, your boss may be in charge of evaluating your performance in a job they've never done and never will do. They might not even fully understand your job. To make matters more frustrating, they may even need to use an evaluation framework designed by someone whom neither of you have met, and who has no understanding of your entire department.

I recently got a front-row seat to this uninformed performance review dynamic at a nationwide fast-casual restaurant. I wasn't at this restaurant as a consultant. I was there to silently work on this book, hoping an environment outside of my office would jump-start my thinking.

The jump-start came in an unexpected way. As I sat in a booth, diligently clicking away on my laptop, the manager of the restaurant and someone who appeared to be from corporate sat down in the adjacent booth.

That's when the store manager's performance review began. To be clear, I didn't have my ear up to a back door or stay past closing time. They sat down next to me in the middle of the restaurant, at 4 p.m. Having said that, once I saw what was happening, I kept my AirPods in and turned my music off . . . for research purposes.

After some pleasantries, they dove into the review. The woman from corporate handed the manager a packet of information: where he stood on certain metrics, his targets for the next quarter, new guidelines for procedures, and ultimately, his pay raise. Overall, his performance was deemed satisfactory, but as the boss went down the list of metrics, tearing in deeper with each line item, the positivity evaporated.

The first point of contention was a metric around paper use. From the context, I assume this means napkins, to-go containers, bags, etc.

Disagree and Commit

The restaurant was 6% over their targeted use. The manager tried to justify his store's overage on metric saying, *This is the South; people are generally not as environmentally conscious.* The woman from corporate wasn't having it: *there are things you can do.* The manager snapped back: *what, like saying "no" when someone asks for extra napkins?*

She didn't have an answer. She moved on to an equally granular line item; the manager was over budget by $200 in office expenses. He told her that he held a contest with his team for upsells, the prize was a $50 gift card and there was a winner every week. The woman from corporate disputed: *couldn't it be a $25 gift card? We need to get this number down.*

In the end, the manager got a raise for his overall good performance. Yet, there he sat, completely defeated. Having been chewed out by someone who had likely never done his job, berated over metrics he could not entirely control, with little mention of the thousands of things he did right.

This back-and-forth played out for well over an hour.

Does it sound familiar? This dynamic happens in restaurants, startups, and Fortune 500s alike.

Hopefully, your performance reviews aren't in the open company of your team and customers (literally insane). Even if they're in a closed office, with your supportive boss, you've likely been subject to a seemingly senseless edict from "above."

In a way, I understood where the corporate woman was coming from. I assume she's responsible for the same metrics, probably an aggregate of a certain geography of stores. Every store counts.

Ironically, this restaurant is founded on a purpose, touting a welcoming and supportive work environment on their career site. Was either party in that review having a particularly purpose-driven experience? No. They both left pissed.

This didn't happen because either party had malicious intent and it didn't happen because the organization had a degrading experience in mind when designing the review process.

This dynamic plays out because of a simple concept I call the concrete cascade. The more cut and dried something is, the easier it is to communicate through an organization. The more abstract something is, the more increasingly difficult it is to communicate it (see Figure 9.1).

Nuances like intent, purpose, and exceptions are exponentially more difficult to cascade than something like a metric, a policy, or action items. Their abstractness leaves too much room for interpretation. People often choose not to cascade them, because it's too difficult, or they cascade them poorly.

When the corporate overlords start barking, their intent isn't (usually) to make your life more difficult. They're falling into the trap of the concrete cascade, and likely not communicating the rationale, intent, and aspirational elements surrounding the granular point of discussion. Often, all that lands on your desk is the metric, to-do, or procedural output.

Figure 9.1 Concrete cascade.

Disagree and Commit

Sometimes, all you can do is safeguard your own headspace, nod through whatever is being said, and assume good intent. (Flip back to Chapter 4 for tips on responding to change.) Other times, you may choose to fight with righteous indignation.

Determining Your Hill to Die On

You've no doubt played (or at least heard of) the game Telephone as a kid. You whisper something in your friend's ear, they whisper what they heard in another friend's ear, and the chain continues through however big your group is. At the end, the last person in the chain says what they heard aloud.

For example, the first person starts out saying "I think broccoli is gross!" and the last person hears (and then says aloud) "I hate boys the most!" It's obvious that the message was completely distorted after it was initially said. Hilarious!

Little did we know this game was training for communicating in the corporate world, where hearing a completely different message at the end of the chain is markedly less funny.

When these edicts are communicated, before you act at all, it's imperative to assess their accuracy. Especially at first, details are often lost in communication. Winding yourself up over a small element is usually a waste of emotional labor.

Mentally place your gut reaction to the side. You can always pick it up later. Lean into asking questions about the intent and the impact of the decision you disagree with:

- What does this mean for me?
- How will my day-to-day change?
- Is this decision or change intentionally designed to make my life more difficult?
- What are the long-term consequences of this for me? My team? This organization?

- How will this impact my boss? Our customers?

- How long did it take to reach this decision? How long will the decision last?

Through this analysis, your gut reaction may prove incorrect. You may elect to just suck it up. Alternatively, you could conclude that you're very right, and choose to die on that hill.

Take a look at Figure 9.2 and try to categorize your most recent corporate edict.

My aim for this grid is to help you see that the majority of organizations don't make decisions out of poor intent. Someone usually made the call because they wanted to do the right thing for the most amount of people, not because they wanted you personally to have more work or leave the office grumpy.

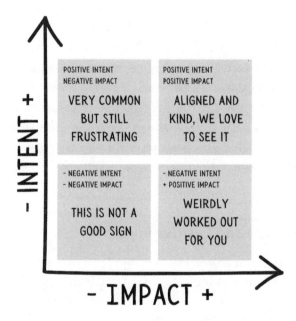

Figure 9.2 Intent and impact.

Positive Intent and Positive Impact

Your organization made a great call and it worked out for you. Yay! Relish in the alignment and put it in the bank of goodwill you have for the company you work for.

Positive Intent and Negative Impact

This is a very common category. Your organization wants to outpace a competitor, launch a new product, or safeguard themselves against a threat. The intent is all there . . . but more work, re-work, or some other headache lands on *your* desk as a result. Oftentimes, the ripple effect of these top-level decisions isn't fully considered. If this happens to you, it might be a decent hill worth dying on. If you choose to push back, try this:

- **Validate the good intent.** You want this organization to thrive too! You care about the outcomes beyond your job.

- **Ask before you assume.** Do you know the full context? Is there something you might not be considering?

- **Present the facts.** Remember, this was concocted with good intent. Using language like "I'd be remiss if I didn't share . . ." or "Based on my role, I'd suggest . . ." Softer language is less combative and gives you an easier out if there is something you missed. It also solidifies your position as a team player, if you will actually experience a negative impact, but the decision is still correct for the organization at large.

Negative Intent and Positive Impact

The decision-maker had bad intentions, but somehow, it weirdly worked out for you. Take the win at the moment, but recognize that negative intent generally doesn't end with a "win" in the long term. If decisions are being made maliciously (like deceiving customers, lying to employees, or cutting the wrong corners) keep an eyebrow raised. It's all but guaranteed it won't indefinitely land in the "positive impact" category for you, even if it is right now.

Negative Intent and Negative Impact

Consider: Is this an isolated event? Is it a pattern? Was this decision made by a new leader? Are more decisions like this going to follow? This thought line will enable you to explore the level of severity. A one-off bad leader or a spitefully made decision happens occasionally. It doesn't mean the organization (or you) are destined for doom. Yet, when someone (or a company) shows you who they are repeatedly, and continues making bad decisions, it's best to walk away clean while you still can.

You Always Get to Decide One Thing: Your Response

Having to move forward with decisions you don't make is part of working for someone else. It is the trade-off you make for a stable salary, resources, support, and the ability to not be in charge of things you'd prefer not to be in charge of, like finance or IT.

The benefit of working alone is you're in charge of everything. That's also the downside (take it from someone who spent four hours on the phone with GoDaddy this month despite having zero technical expertise).

Ultimately, you might decide the disagree and commit lifestyle isn't for you. Departing the corporate world may be a trade-off you're willing to make. We'll talk more about that in Chapter 12.

In transparency, leaving the corporate world for more autonomy was a decision that I personally made. Having said that, I underestimated the value of big company perks, like having someone to set up your laptop, cover for you when you're sick, and direct deposit the same amount in your bank account every other Friday.

You're probably never going to deliver the speech you gave so passionately in the shower. The executive team won't apologize to you and finally acknowledge your unprecedented genius. The work will go on and the potential alternatives to this decision will likely be forgotten. You can choose to view that truth as defeating or freeing.

When we're up against a decision we believe is wrong, it can be challenging to fend off resentment and frustration. It's a natural response, but if you lean into it, you will be the only one paying the price.

You weren't in charge of making the decision (though that doesn't mean you can't impact it or reverse it). You're in charge of you and how you respond. Be all in, or do yourself and your company a favor, and be all out. Longstanding, unspoken resentment is never the right choice.

REMEMBER

- THE ABILITY TO MOVE FORWARD WITH A PLAN YOU'RE NOT ENTIRELY IN AGREEMENT WITH IS A HALLMARK OF A HIGH PERFORMER AND GOOD TEAMMATE. IT'S ALSO IMPERATIVE FOR NOT GOING INSANE IN THE CORPORATE WORLD, WHERE YOU WILL INEVITABLY DISAGREE WITH MANY DECISIONS YOUR ORGANIZATION MAKES.

- HOLDING YOUR BREATH WAITING TO BE PROVEN RIGHT DOESN'T SERVE YOUR ORGANIZATION, AND MORE IMPORTANTLY, IT DOESN'T SERVE YOU. IT KEEPS YOU EMOTIONALLY ON GUARD AND RELUCTANT TO LEAN IN.

- YOU CAN RESPECTFULLY PUSH BACK ON A DECISION BY VALIDATING THE GOOD INTENT AND PRESENTING THE FACTS WITH HELPFUL, SOFT LANGUAGE.

Chapter 10

Feedback Without the Awkwardness

"When I said 'I am open to feedback,' I meant you could pay me a compliment . . ."

—Sarah Hass

In 2016, I shot my first video course with LinkedIn Learning (then Lynda .com). I agonized over scripts, most videos took several takes, and the end product, while definitely decent, was admittedly a little awkward on my end.

Over the next six years, I created 20 more courses on topics like talent retention, employee engagement, finding purpose at work, and the very first version of Leading Yourself. I had gotten to the point of being able to write great scripts quickly. I could often film videos in a single take. My delivery was more conversational and personable. Thanks to great coaching from producers, directors, and even the teleprompter operator, I got a lot better.

After wrapping up a recent shoot, the producer I was working with gave me what was intended to be an exceptional compliment. Here's what she said:

> I went back and watched your very first course from 2016. I can't believe how much you've grown as an instructor. You're so much more fluid, your delivery is smoother, and I can tell you're more comfortable. It's a night and day difference!

It's a comment that should've made me feel great. Yet, somehow, it made me feel terrible.

> Have you ever had the experience? When you're praised for improvement, and instead of feeling proud of your growth, you're embarrassed about your original state? It's a common conundrum for high performers.

I've been in somewhat of a unique position having to deal with an overabundance of "feedback." When most people's professional growth gets buried in some internal server, my early efforts are still living on the internet for anyone to see, at any time. Plus, anyone with a LinkedIn account can leave a review on my courses.

Through years of mass commentary on my work, I've gotten a lot better at receiving feedback. I've learned to see the grain of truth in poorly presented criticism and my growth mindset has evolved. While you may occasionally still find me stewing about a particular comment, especially when I know the person is right, negative feedback burns less than it used to. I've also learned what to take and what to ignore.

Managing feedback is a foundational element for anyone who wants to lead themselves. Being able to give feedback, receive it (even when poorly presented), and choose whether or not to act on it plays a significant role in your growth trajectory.

Asking for Feedback: A Lesson from Cartoonists

Have you ever had an idea you loved, and your boss immediately started poking holes in it? Have you ever created a presentation only to have your colleagues respond with a list of things you should add?

It's not because your work is inherently poor. It's because as humans, we're instinctively wired to want to point out flaws and try to make improvements. And the ambitious people in your company are even more eager to put their mark on any new developments than most.

The secret is giving all those well-intended critics a place to weigh in.

In graphic design, they call this the "hairy arms" phenomenon. Here's how it played out at Disney, according to Jessica Frease, a graphic designer:[1]

> So the story goes that probably a long while ago – probably in the '30s or '40s – Disney had lead animators, but they also had creative directors. And when the lead animators would make concept designs, meaning, like, character development, they'd be so proud of these characters. And they would go to their art directors, and their art directors would change something constantly.

Sound familiar? You do great work and bring it to someone (usually your boss) who wants to put their own spin on things. Here's where it gets interesting.

Frease continues,

> So what they did was to distract the directors from making other changes, they would automatically add hair on the arms of each character. Then, they would bring it into the big meeting with all the head honchos. And those guys would say "oh, well, you've got to get rid of the hair on the arms" . . . That's where the term "hairy arms" comes from.

Even though the animators knew having hair on the cartoon's arms looked ridiculous, they added it anyway, because they wanted to give the big boss a way to change something, without taking away from the original vision for the character.

Should you try to manipulate your boss or peers by including the proverbial "hairy arms" in your work product? Not exactly. As tempting as it may be to intentionally misalign slides or include a glaringly obvious typo, this practice can cost you what might be valuable feedback. Instead, you want to point feedback-givers in the most productive directions. In an ideal world, your boss's and peers' brains are working to provide a meaningful response (versus succumbing to a little trick).

They're going to want to contribute; it's your job to show them *how*.

163

Feedback Without the Awkwardness

To lead yourself, you need valuable feedback along the way.

To get that valuable feedback, there are three important elements of the feedback equation to optimize: timing, strength, and scope. Guardrails on each ensure the most valuable feedback possible is received at the exact moment it's needed.

Here's how you can put your own parameters on these three elements to get better and more helpful feedback on your work.

Timing

Waiting until you deem your work absolutely perfect before asking for feedback is setting you and the feedback-giver up for failure. The more time marches on, the more intellectual horsepower you spend refining, the less open you're going to be.

Think about the technology you use every day: Zoom, iCloud, Gmail, whatever it is. Each one of those platforms launched a beta version first. Tech companies *know* that no matter how much time their organization spends fine-tuning each feature, it's not going to be perfect. A fresh perspective and outside lens will almost always change something.

The same is true on a smaller scale, for your work. Asking for feedback on your beta version is more helpful than waiting until you're done. Even if you don't get clear actionable feedback, something someone said can further prompt your thinking (if you're open to it).

That's why it's crucial to not wait until the last second to ask for feedback. Instead, pick a few interim junctures where feedback would be helpful. This might be after you outline a project plan or create an initial draft. Early feedback is easier to assess and easier to act on. Remember, you can always reject the feedback . . . but you won't get to make that decision if you don't ask.

Strength

We talked in Chapter 8 about knowing what your boss is good at. The same is true with your peers and even your customers.

For example, let's say your colleague has an exceptional eye for detail. Asking for their feedback in the brainstorming stages is probably going to be a frustrating experience for you both. They're going to be wondering why your color palette isn't on-brand and you're going to be wondering why they can't be free-thinking this early in the process. Your colleague feels like you aren't valuing their advice (they're right), and you feel like your colleague isn't supporting you in development (you're right). In that scenario, you'd likely get better feedback (and have a more enjoyable experience) by bouncing ideas off of one of your more creative-brained colleagues first.

Knowing someone's strengths enables you to leverage those strengths most effectively. That might read a little manipulative; it's not intended to be. People deserve to have their expertise valued. They should be asked to contribute where their brain can be most useful. And you deserve the most helpful, constructive feedback possible. Tapping into someone's innate strengths in the feedback equation serves all parties.

Personally, if you ask for my help on copyediting, it's going to be a really frustrating experience for both of us. I'll hate the process and you'll still end up with typos. If you ask for my help designing a new training program, we're both going to have fun, and I'm confident I can help you come up with something creative.

Scope

When asked for feedback, most people *will* come up with something to change or add. It's your job to point them to where they can be most helpful. Throwing a lengthy proposal or massive deck at someone for "feedback" is almost never a good idea. It's going to take them tons of time and their feedback is more likely to be unhelpful to you.

Alternatively, asking for feedback on something specific, like the timing, pricing, or graphics, points their eye and gives their mind a place to land. The clearer you can be about the feedback you're looking for, the more efficient and effective your feedback giver can be (again, respectful to them, no one wants to waste their time *and* be unhelpful).

Another subtle benefit of a defined feedback scope is you're less likely to get a blanket "looks great!" At first blush, that might not sound like a benefit . . . because "looks great" is a nice compliment. However, an undefined scope can leave the feedback-giver overwhelmed. They don't know how detailed of feedback you want, if they're off-base by bringing something up, or if it's too late . . . so they keep their thoughts to themselves, usually to be courteous. This dynamic causes you to miss out on what could be valuable feedback.

The scope you're defining should be informed by the person's strengths and the timing of the feedback. Another consideration for your requested scope is asking for feedback on the areas where you're actively struggling.

A Clear Ask

A clear feedback ask could look something like:

> I'm writing a proposal for a new prospect. I'm planning to send it at the end of the month. Of course, the proposal is going to be passed around by the customer and I won't be there to answer questions every time someone reads it. I know you worked with a similar client last year. Could you read the objectives section of this and let me know if the goals are clear?

That request for feedback leverages the three elements I described earlier:

- **Timing.** This proposal is still in the development stage, and thus, feedback won't send the asker into a mental tailspin. The feedback-giver also knows they have some time to work with; it's not too late.

- **Strength.** The feedback giver's strengths are validated – they worked with a similar client last year. This is a thoughtful request, not a thrown-around favor.

- **Scope.** The objective section is important, in line with the strengths of the feedback-giver, and where the feedback-asker is struggling. They don't need to read every word of the proposal to provide feedback.

The more you optimize the timing, the strengths, and the scope in your feedback equation the more likely you are to get feedback that's actually useful (even if it stings a little at first).

The Feedback Behind the Feedback

People don't always give good advice. To lead yourself, you'll need to extrapolate good advice from random opinions.

When you get feedback, it's tempting to think you only have two choices: Take the feedback or ignore it.

There's a third choice, and it's the most powerful of all: Look behind it.

In screenwriting, a mentor or producer will provide "notes" to writers on their scripts. It's the film industry term for feedback. As background, writers are known to be fairly sensitive about their work. I say this as a writer. Creative expressions are vulnerable, the work can be highly personal, and feedback is generally a matter of personal opinion – versus an obvious bug in code or a miscalculation on a spreadsheet.

In this scenario, it would be easy to discount a "note" that conflicts with your creative vision. But here's what screenwriters are taught in the early days: look for the note behind the note.

Why was that feedback given? What's behind it that's not being said?

For example, perhaps a script note says, "This scene feels inauthentic." What's the note behind the note? Perhaps up until now, the main character hasn't been very likable. They haven't shown any vulnerability, made any mistakes, or said anything that made them relatable. It might not necessarily be a problem with the scene itself; it was all of the dialogue (or lack thereof) that led up to it.

Sometimes feedback givers don't really know the "why" behind their feedback. That doesn't mean the feedback is wrong.

You've probably watched a film, walked through a model home, or read a report that was off somehow. You didn't know why, but you knew it was off. The people giving you feedback are much the same; they may be giving you a first reaction without knowing why they feel that way.

Ideally, the feedback-giver has contextualized their remarks and walked you through what led them to that conclusion. In the event they don't (they probably won't), you can uncover the feedback behind the feedback by asking questions like:

- What prompted that thinking?
- Why do you think that jumped out at you?
- Do you think that's emblematic of this project/idea/problem?
- How can I build on that?
- How can I resolve that?
- In your eyes, what should change?
- What would happen if I changed that?
- Have you had a similar experience/worked on a similar project that went differently?

This isn't an interrogation or an attempt to invalidate the feedback. You're genuinely curious: What's behind this? Is it deeper than the initial feedback suggests?

After you establish some more context, you may choose to push back. In fact there's some interesting research from entrepreneurship scholar Susan Cohen that suggests that pushing back in the moment will actually get you better advice. After analyzing 165 conversations between entrepreneurs and their mentors, Cohen and her fellow researchers (Amisha Miller and Siobhan O'Mahony) found a stark difference between entrepreneurs who took the advice with a head nod versus those who challenged it.

In her TEDx talk,[2] Cohen shares an example from the founders of a startup that made snacks from fruit and vegetable pulp. Pulp is the stringy, fibrous part of the fruit (insane people like it in orange juice).

The founders of the pulp snack were originally targeting moms and juice shops. Their mentors suggested that their target market was too narrow, recommending they sell to grocery stores instead. The founders pushed back: "We can't mass market by telling people they're eating waste!"

By pushing back in the moment, the founders invited their mentors to help them come up with a better way to talk about fruit waste. They ultimately called it "The healthiest part of the fruit." It worked. Mainstream shoppers did eat the (rebranded) pulp snacks from a grocery store.

Another interesting note, across the entire study, was that the founders who politely acknowledged their mentor's advice with a "Thank you! Interesting!" pleasantry, never actually used the advice later. Only the founders who pushed back actually used the advice.

But here's the kicker: Those founders didn't use the advice exactly as it was initially given. While their counterparts were nodding and saying thank you, these founders were actively engaging with their mentors, asking them to clarify advice, asking for more details, and adapting it through a collaborative conversation. The advice was cocreated, instead of doled out. The outcome was driven by active participation from the advice recipient.

Before you politely nod and ignore feedback, or openly deny any validity, consider:

- You might be getting feedback on something that isn't ready for feedback (like the early bud of a big idea) or is too cemented (like your heart and soul final version).

- There might be valuable feedback behind the feedback that you're missing.

- The seed of the advice could be good and would benefit from polite pushback.

When you're leading yourself, it's helpful to approach feedback with a mindset of curiosity. Seek to understand before you decide if it's advice worth taking.

I learned a shortcut for doing this from Dorie Clark, the author of *The Long Game*, whom I referenced earlier in this book. She suggests using the blanket "Tell me more." This helps the other person see that they're not under attack, you're not being defensive, and you're truly trying to understand.

As you move through your career, there will be no shortage of people who are willing to give you advice (me included, I guess). It won't all be good for you, no matter how well intended. No one knows your reality, your goals, and your vision like you do.

Whether the feedback is coming from your boss, a colleague, a customer, or a random stranger writing a book, what you take from it is yours to decide.

Norman Vincent Peale famously said, "The trouble with most of us is that we would rather be ruined by praise than saved by criticism." While praise certainly feels better than criticism, people who are most effective at leading themselves don't shy away from hearing hard truths.

Assess, Don't Obsess

Feedback can be very valuable. It's also something high-performing people and organizations obsess over, sometimes to the point of detriment.

Culturally, we've never been asked for more feedback than we are now. You're asked for feedback on your DoorDash delivery, your Amazon purchase, the time you spent with Tech Support, and seemingly every other time you buy something or interact with anyone (even the automated "help" bot). We live in a world that tells us every opinion matters, especially yours. Our colleagues and company also got the same memo.

While you want to do great work and make a point of asking for feedback, you'll want to watch out for three common feedback-obsession traps.

Trap 1: Over-Asking

The constant "we want your feedback" narrative has made its way into the employer-employee dynamic, too. Not long ago, I worked with an organization that sent out an employee survey every two weeks. It's a well-intended strategy: the leaders ask for feedback because they want their employees to be engaged, and cared for, and to stay with the organization. But asking every two weeks was sabotaging the quality of feedback.

Over-asking for feedback tends to result in a myriad of challenges:

- **The person or people you're asking get annoyed.** Asking for feedback is an *ask*. When someone is over-asked, they inevitably get frustrated, especially if it feels like they're giving feedback into a void, which is often the case with employee surveys. Because two weeks isn't enough time to substantially change anything, the following survey will likely be the same, which diminishes the confidence of the feedback giver that there is any point in giving feedback at all.

- **The feedback is disproportionately weighted to the now.** If you think to yourself, "Do I like this job?" every day, the days when your job is frustrating are going to feel a lot more consequential than they actually are. You answer a resounding "No! I'm not engaged!" because Phil from engineering really pissed you off this morning.

- **The overall quality of feedback goes down.** By sheer feedback exhaustion, the clarity and robustness of the feedback are going to diminish. People are never more eager to give feedback than the first time they're asked.

The cost of over-asking plays out on an organizational level *and* an individual level. Imagine if your spouse asks you every day: Are you mad at me? Did I do something wrong? How am I doing as a spouse? Are you sure you're happy? At first, you're likely to appreciate the check-in. Eventually, you'll find a reason to say no. The laundry they left on the floor that you initially brushed off that morning is now a point of contention.

You're annoyed, the feedback is disproportionately weighted to the now, and the quality of the feedback (because it's disproportionately weighted and delivered in an annoyed tone) is not helpful.

Over-asking tends to cater more to ranting than it does constructive feedback. If you ask for feedback on every little thing, you'll get (probably unhelpful) feedback on every little thing. Plus if you ask for enough feedback from enough people, the feedback is even going to start conflicting with itself, which makes "what to do with the feedback" even more confusing.

171

Feedback Without the Awkwardness

Trap 2: Failing to Consider the Source

All feedback is not equal (despite sometimes appearing in the same spreadsheet). In an era of feedback overwhelm, it can be challenging to differentiate the feedback from an informed source versus a random disgruntled comment.

There's something to be said for anonymous feedback. This practice can enable feedback without fear of repercussions.

It's also true that someone who can't "do the thing" can provide helpful feedback. For example: Can I give tattoos? No. Can I point out one with shaky lines? Yes. You probably can too.

Having said that, it's generally wise to consider the source before acting on significant feedback.

I was chatting with my neighbor who is a director for the CDC. Her team had recently gotten a new executive leader and people had their opinions. Their former leader was loose with deadlines and not very organized. As a result, the team's performance wasn't exactly stellar. This new leader, in stark contrast, ran a tight ship, which wasn't received well by a team that had only recently had very low expectations with minimal accountability.

As a mature mid-level leader, who has seen many bosses come and go, she described the team's griping by saying, "When people complain about someone else, I'm always paying attention to who is doing the complaining. It's often lazy people complaining about someone holding them accountable, rude people complaining about an expectation of courteousness, or disorganized people complaining about the need for any sort of order."

Her ability to consider the source applies to any type of feedback. Considering the source can help you avoid over-indexing on feedback from underqualified people. You can consider the source by reflecting on questions like:

- Is this person able to demonstrate themselves what they're asking of you?

- Has this person been able to improve, grow, and evolve themselves?

- Are they receptive to feedback? Or do they only dish it out?

- Do they have experience or expertise in this area?

- Have they provided helpful feedback in the past? Even to other people?
- Is their intention with this feedback to help me and my work improve?

If the answer to all of those is a resounding no, it's worth reconsidering whether their feedback is even valid. It's certainly less valuable than something that comes from someone with actual expertise. If someone is constantly poking holes in your work and they do that to *everyone*, about *everything*, their hole-poking is more likely to be an unfortunate personality trait than it is a useful critique. Don't lose too much sleep over it.

Trap 3: Over-Indexing on Negative Feedback

I went to college at the peak of "Rate my Professor." People often picked their classes based on what former students had to say about the instructor. There were rankings for the level of difficulty, the quality of the class, and even how physically attractive the professor was (though thankfully the website doesn't include that category anymore).

Now, people often rate their peers, their boss, literally everything. Organizations get rated as employers on Glassdoor, individuals get endorsed by their colleagues on LinkedIn, and companies get evaluated by their customers on every social media site imaginable.

Whether you're getting feedback or giving feedback, there's a tendency to over-index on negative feedback. People with neutral experiences or even good experiences are less inclined to share them.

Here's how the over-indexing on negative feedback trap often plays out:

- You ask for feedback from six of your colleagues. One person brings up a challenge in your work. You re-do the whole thing to cater to that one piece of negative feedback, ignoring that five people found the initial work to be completely fine.

- You read a negative piece of feedback about a potential employer. You show up to the interview cautious and guarded, having no idea what the other 100+ employees think. That single piece of negative feedback, from someone who may have been justly fired, keeps you from showing up with enthusiasm and energy.

- You're asked to give feedback to your teammate on an important proposal. It's overall good, but the pricing they've laid out is confusing. You shared that with them. They fix the pricing, but now, their confidence is low, because you didn't validate the parts that were actually good.

That last one hurts because we've all done it. We ignore the good and give feedback on the bad because we want to be helpful, further perpetuating the over-index on the negative trap.

My favorite college professor, Professor Craig Sender, who I mentioned earlier, had zero reviews on Rate My Professor when I signed up for his class. Had there been even one negative review, I wouldn't have been as optimistic on the first day. Had there been a few negative reviews (despite hundreds of students who left no reviews), I likely would've picked a different professor.

What's worse than me missing out on a great experience is that had he gotten a negative review from a constantly disgruntled student, he may have been tempted to change his approach, potentially for the worse.

When you over-index on negative feedback, you lose sight of all of the positive elements no one went out of their way to mention. You don't see the existing strength in your work and you don't see it in other people's, either.

Assess, don't obsess.

Don't Make Other People Pay the Price for Your Discomfort

When I brought up giving people a defined scope when asking for feedback, I mentioned the risk of a blanket "looks great!" Many people *want* to give positive feedback much more than they want to give constructive feedback. It feels good to pass out compliments.

While I've learned to take feedback like a champ (most of the time), giving feedback is still something I struggle with. I routinely find myself tempted to beat around the bush when it comes to doling out constructive criticism, even when I'm literally hired to provide these kinds of critiques.

The temptation to avoid giving constructive feedback is natural, and becomes even stronger in the face of a few factors:

- **The person asking for feedback is someone who has (actual or perceived) authority over you.** They're your boss, they've been with the company longer, you deem them smarter, more creative, whatever it is. The power dynamic can stifle your voice.

- **You know the feedback is going to hurt a little, no matter how thoughtfully you deliver it.** When the person is really proud of what they created, when they've been working on it for a long time, when they positively beam upon showing you . . . it's tougher to speak up.

- **The organizational culture around feedback is punitive.** If "feedback" is synonymous with "wrong" and the only acceptable state is "perfect," the feedback conversation can become fraught quickly. Over time, people learn to avoid the conversation entirely by saying "looks great!" (when it doesn't).

The most common scenario is when your manager asks for your feedback. Unless your working relationship is absolutely stellar, you're probably at least a little bit tempted to bite your tongue, deflecting to some version of "I love it! You're a genius! Great work! Wow!"

That's not helpful (or kind) to your boss. In the long term, it erodes trust.

What if they move forward with a bad presentation, only to find out that you thought it was bad and didn't tell them? What if you knew their calculations were off but let it go anyway, and then they had to spend all weekend reworking the numbers?

Brenda Fridman, a LinkedIn sales leader, summed this up for me in one of her posts, saying: "Holding back valuable feedback is equivalent to deliberately sabotaging someone's career."

When you know you need to give the maybe-uncomfortable but definitely

> If someone is asking you for feedback, they're asking because they value your expertise and they trust you have their back. Don't prove them wrong.

necessary feedback . . . how do you do it in a way that doesn't make the other person hate you?

Walk the other person through your thought process and help them understand why you have this feedback. You're not throwing a blind critique of this person's work. You're offering a perspective that would help them. Take a look at the examples in Figure 10.1.

It seems counterintuitive, but explaining your thought process shows your feedback is coming with good intent. You're not just taking cheap shots; you thoughtfully reached this conclusion and you're trying to help.

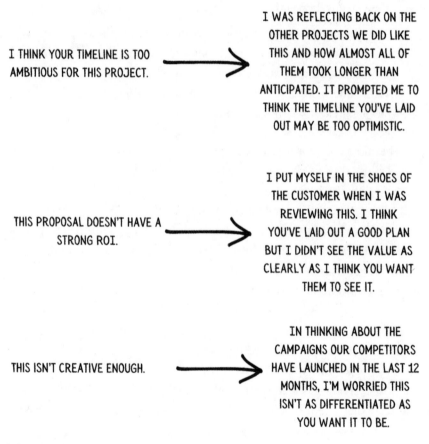

I THINK YOUR TIMELINE IS TOO AMBITIOUS FOR THIS PROJECT. → I WAS REFLECTING BACK ON THE OTHER PROJECTS WE DID LIKE THIS AND HOW ALMOST ALL OF THEM TOOK LONGER THAN ANTICIPATED. IT PROMPTED ME TO THINK THE TIMELINE YOU'VE LAID OUT MAY BE TOO OPTIMISTIC.

THIS PROPOSAL DOESN'T HAVE A STRONG ROI. → I PUT MYSELF IN THE SHOES OF THE CUSTOMER WHEN I WAS REVIEWING THIS. I THINK YOU'VE LAID OUT A GOOD PLAN BUT I DIDN'T SEE THE VALUE AS CLEARLY AS I THINK YOU WANT THEM TO SEE IT.

THIS ISN'T CREATIVE ENOUGH. → IN THINKING ABOUT THE CAMPAIGNS OUR COMPETITORS HAVE LAUNCHED IN THE LAST 12 MONTHS, I'M WORRIED THIS ISN'T AS DIFFERENTIATED AS YOU WANT IT TO BE.

Figure 10.1 Thought process feedback delivery.

We all remember the person who saved us from ourselves – everything from politely pointing out that you have something in your teeth to asking more questions when the financials of a new business venture aren't adding up.

Even when it's uncomfortable in the moment, giving feedback is an important element of being a good colleague, friend, and human being.

Leading yourself means interacting with others in a way that you want them to interact with you. Whatever side of the feedback equation you're on, you can fend off awkwardness with intentionality.

REMEMBER

- PEOPLE WANT TO CONTRIBUTE; IT'S YOUR JOB TO SHOW THEM HOW. OPTIMIZE THE TIMING OF YOUR FEEDBACK REQUEST, DEFINE THE SCOPE, AND HARNESS THE STRENGTHS OF THE PERSON YOU'RE ASKING.

- EVEN FEEDBACK THAT'S POORLY PRESENTED CAN BE BENEFICIAL. DIG BENEATH CONFUSING OR VAGUE FEEDBACK BY ASKING QUESTIONS AND SEEKING TO UNDERSTAND.

- ASSESS, DON'T OBSESS. ASKING FOR FEEDBACK TOO OFTEN OR TAKING ALL FEEDBACK TOO SERIOUSLY WILL ERODE YOUR MORALE AND WEAKEN YOUR RESULTS.

- DON'T MAKE OTHER PEOPLE PAY THE PRICE FOR YOUR DISCOMFORT. IF YOU HAVE CONSTRUCTIVE FEEDBACK THAT WILL HELP THE OTHER PERSON, PRESENT IT KINDLY AND WALK THEM THROUGH YOUR THOUGHT PROCESS.

Chapter 11

All Those Other People

"What did our mothers teach us? Treat others as you want to be treated. Excellent advice and very well-intentioned. And it works, too – as long as everyone is just like you."

—Thomas Erikson, *Surrounded by Idiots.*

The working world is a group project that never ends.

Your relationships with your colleagues will, for better or worse, have a major impact on your career. While you may get your own performance review, their success and yours are likely intertwined. At least for now.

To lead yourself, you'll need to be able to work well with a pretty big variety of people.

Just like you decide whether you get married, travel the world, prioritize your health, or whatever else, everyone gets to make their own choices about their level of perfectionism, ambition, and benevolence. They can differ from your choices and not be a moral failing.

Though when your colleagues start to ghost your emails, fail to deliver, or take their childhood trauma out on you . . . something must be done.

The Misery of Unmet Expectations

In almost a decade of consulting, I've seen a lot of strained working relationships. I've been a part of a few, too. Almost all tense working relationships stem from a single root cause: unmet expectations.

It doesn't matter whether the expectations were clearly defined and agreed upon or not. It doesn't even matter if they're reasonable expectations at all. If an expectation is unmet, especially repeatedly, there's tension.

This could look like:

- Your boss thinks you should answer emails on Sunday night. You don't think that. Neither of you express your email expectations. You're annoyed they're emailing you. They're annoyed you're not answering.

- You and Stan are working on an onboarding project together. For you, this is a priority. For Stan, it's a project he thought sounded doable but realistically he didn't have time for it. You assume Stan is a slacker who can't prioritize. Stan thinks you're a try-hard who believes this is more important than it is.

- Based on your last team, you assume you'll develop friendships with your colleagues in a new job. Your new colleagues aren't friends with each other and they don't seem to want to be friends with you. You think they're standoffish. They think you're unprofessional.

So much workplace angst traces back to people not saying, doing, or behaving the way we expect them to. The good news is, you can avoid a lot of this "unmet expectations" disgruntledness by clearly defining expectations and accurately predicting when they'll be unmet.

Defining Expectations (Without Being a Jerk)

Defining the expectations of people who work for you is fairly straightforward. You strike a balance between giving autonomy and support, you're clear with deadlines and parameters, and if you have a good team, you can expect things to go relatively smoothly.

Setting expectations is more complex when no one is "in charge." And potentially even more weird when you're setting expectations upward – to your boss.

Expectations aren't always an explicit conversation. Expectations are set by your behavior, every day, in lots of small ways. What you do, don't do, and how you respond define the expectation of what it's like to work with you.

Here are some examples of how that plays out:

> To lead yourself (and still work well with the people around you), ground yourself in this simple truth: You teach people how to treat you.

- The more you take evening calls, the more you'll get them. And people will expect you to answer. As more time passes, they'll be pissed when you don't.

- The more you "no problem!" all of your colleagues when they don't deliver what they're responsible for, the more they'll internalize that it's never a problem to let you down.

- The more you bail out your boss at the last second, the more they'll expect it.

- The more you "bounce this to the top of their inbox" or "friendly reminder" people on deadlines, the more they'll assume you'll remind them, even if that's not your job.

Of course, there are extenuating circumstances. You'll have to bail your boss out sometimes, just like they'll probably have to bail you out, too. Emergencies (real ones) do happen, deadlines get missed, and the drumbeat of the numbers marches on.

Just be mindful of behavioral patterns.

I was talking with a new head of HR a couple of years ago. Unsurprisingly, people come to him to air their grievances about their colleagues. So and so missed the deadline, was standoffish in a meeting, isn't answering emails, etc. After a few months, he was overwhelmed with fairly minor but annoying complaints.

The head of HR knew the culture had to change. No one was willing to directly confront someone who was seemingly not meeting expectations. They just complained about it to anyone that would listen.

He implemented a simple response when someone came into his office grumbling about one of their colleagues. The head of HR responded with: *What did they say when you told them?*

It was a sobering response for many because it revealed that the expectation was either not clearly defined *or* if it was defined, the fact the expectation wasn't met isn't being addressed directly with the offender.

So, how can you keep yourself from complaining to HR or being (unknowingly) complained about? Clear expectations. Sometimes, expectations are spelled out, like timelines, who is doing what on a project, budget constraints, and easier-to-define parameters. Those easier-to-define parameters aren't usually the cause of an emotional downfall in a team.

The expectations that are frequently missed (but have a huge impact on your working relationships) are things like:

- How available are we outside of traditional business hours?
- What level of candor is expected when giving feedback?
- How quickly is an email response expected? How quickly are phone calls usually returned?
- What constitutes an urgent problem?
- How will we handle it if we disagree? Does someone have the final say-so? Will we escalate it to a more senior leader?
- What if we need help? What if one of us is unable to do our part? (Emergencies happen.)
- Who is responsible for taking notes in the meeting?

This list isn't meant to be an interrogation to run through during your first meeting; you'll never be able to *perfectly* define working norms because things happen. Keep the prompts in mind and talk about them in the early stages of working together, before you start to get upset that people aren't

Leading Yourself

meeting your expectations. And before other people get upset that you (probably unknowingly) aren't meeting *their* expectations.

If you find yourself thinking "It's assumed that . . ." or "Everyone knows that . . ." catch yourself. It's not assumed. They don't know that.

When the expectations are clear and agreed upon, an unmet expectation becomes factual, instead of personal. Clear expectations make it easier to say "What we initially agreed upon was X. Has something changed?" You remove the angst, assumptions, and tension.

> No one is in your brain except you, and the odds of your entire team (who all have different backgrounds, work styles, and skills) reading your mind are extremely low.

For all you know, something did change! And there's a reason expectations are going unmet. Save yourself from the maddening mental spiral of "they should have known."

In the words of Brené Brown, clear is kind. Spelling it out doesn't make you a jerk. Defining expectations makes you someone who sets your team, your boss, and yourself up for success.

Predicting When Expectations Will Not Be Met

If you were taken hostage, and your captors allotted you one phone call, but the person *had* to pick up, who would you call?

You know who in your life answers the phone and who doesn't.

You also know who in your work life you can count on, and who has a history of not meeting expectations (for whatever reason). You don't have to get angry about it. Accept it as a fact and control the controllable.

Here are three actions you can take when you think someone might let you down:

- **Give them individual autonomy.** This sounds counterintuitive, but a primary driver of someone not delivering is the fact they viewed said "thing" as a "group responsibility." Let's take a lesson from water safety, where a lack of individual ownership can be fatal: 88% of child drownings occur with at least one adult present, and 50% of children drown within 25 yards of a parent or other adult.[1] Why? Because all adults assume the other adults are watching, and when "everyone is watching," no one is watching. Now, in corporate, how does that play out? When everyone is responsible for doing the research, coming up with ideas, following up, etc., no one is responsible for it. Sometimes the person not meeting expectations needs to see that if something goes undone, it's on them, and them alone.

- **Give buffer time.** British scholar Cyril Northcote Parkinson famously said, "Work expands so as to fill the time available for its completion." If you tell someone you need it on Friday, odds are, they're sending it on Friday. If your spidey senses are telling you someone won't deliver, tell them you need it earlier than you do. It's not the nicest tactic but it can be a method of self-protection, and keep you from paying the price when so-and-so inevitably falls short. With the buffer time, you can make a plan B.

- **Tell them you're worried.** Back to the head of HR asking, *what did they say when you told them?* If you're predicting someone won't deliver, and you have a long history informing that belief, tell them. You don't have to say "I'm worried you won't deliver." You can finesse it a little bit, offering an "I know on our last project it was a struggle to do XYZ. I don't want to fall into that pattern again. Is there any reason this won't be done by X due date? Is there any way I can support you?" There's a strong chance this person will pick up what you're putting down, and in a quest to preserve their reputation, they may actually do what you need.

Leading yourself means controlling the controllable. You can't puppeteer your colleagues, but with intentionality and preparation, you can impact their behavior more than you may suspect.

Safeguarding Yourself Against Negativity

It's long been said, *you are who you surround yourself with*. That expression discounts the role of genetics, environmental factors, and the everlasting impact of your own childhood. Still, the people around us have a major impact on how we feel and who we become.

Unfortunately, in an effort to build connection with those around us, we often resort to bonding over negativity. Yes, there are times when we laugh in solidarity at a Dilbert cartoon or collectively sigh in the face of an unreasonable deadline, but constant negativity can leave you feeling drained.

Emotions are contagious, and according to Dr. Sherrie Bourg Carter, "Negativity keeps pounding away at you and ultimately results in significant second-hand stress, which as you might expect, has the same effects on your mind and body as direct stress. The body experiences and interprets it as one and the same."[2]

Here's how the cycle typically plays out at work (see Figure 11.1).

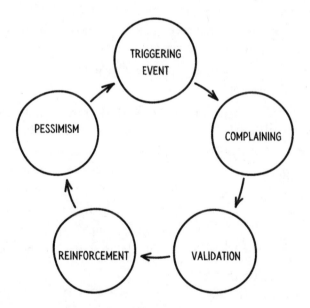

Figure 11.1 Negativity cycle.

Triggering event → complaining → validation → reinforcement → pessimism:

- **Triggering event:** Something annoying happens to your colleague.

- **Complaining:** Your colleague comes to you to gripe about it.

- **Validation:** In an effort to build psychological safety and connection with them, you validate it. "You're right! That sucks!"

- **Reinforcement:** Their beliefs are confirmed. Righteous indignation remains.

- **Pessimism:** They leave. Your mood is worse off.

- **Another triggering event:** Then something annoying happens to you. Of course, it does! And because you just spent your time and mental horsepower grumbling, your annoyance is now magnified, feeding a story of just how annoying everything and everyone is.

Be careful spending too much time with the people who reinforce the negativity cycle. Be even more careful about the role you're playing.

Continuing to nod along to someone's "this is awful" rant or even politely laughing at the 47th "this company sucks" joke reinforces the behavior. If you disagree, say so. Yes, it will be awkward for a few minutes. But that person will eventually stop plunking their negativity down on your desk (or in your inbox).

If you have nurturing tendencies, you may want to help this person feel better. You don't want them to be hopeless, so you offer validation, support, and commiseration. If this doesn't help at first, it probably won't.

Imagine one of your particularly grumbly colleagues shows up to a Zoom meeting with you. You say hello, and ask how their day is going (you already know what they're going to say). "UGH! There's always some change going on here, things are never settled. I'm so tired of the constant disruption!" Instead of the tempting *yeah* . . . response, you counter. You say something like "It's not settled, but I'm excited for the growth ahead!" Maybe a little bit cringy for a second, but the conversation moves on. The next time you ask them how they're doing? They'll reply with "Fine, how are you?"

To break negative cycles, someone needs to be an active participant in their own change. Meet people where they are, not where you wish they were, or even where you know they could be.

Instead of fighting a losing battle to rewire someone else, in most cases, you're better off putting some boundaries up and making a proactive effort to surround yourself with positivity. That's where work friends come in.

Friends at Work

In *Braving the Wilderness*, Brené Brown tells a story of women who lived in a village and would gather by the river to wash their clothes together. As time marched on, the women moved on to the latest technology – washing machines – and not long after they all got washing machines, the rates of depression in the village increased.

When the women stopped gathering by the river to do the washing, they lost connection, a sense of belonging, and community that came with the chore. It was a devastating consequence that no one anticipated, simply by upgrading a chore as old as time.[3]

Humans are inherently social creatures. We cannot survive alone. We live in families, work in teams, and gather in fellowship. I'm not suggesting you and your boss head down to the river to wash your clothes, but you should build time in your work day for connection with your colleagues. Potentially even friendship.

There's an old-school belief that to be professional, you shouldn't be friends with your colleagues, much less your subordinates or boss.

The notion of "no friends at work" was likely propelled by a generation of leaders who operated in a rigid hierarchy, under-indexing on empathy, compassion, and sometimes basic human decency. Unsurprisingly, they weren't making a lot of friends at the office.

This historical thinking drastically underestimates the nuance and maturity most humans are capable of. The current research tells us friendship has huge benefits at work. Leading yourself is not a sentence to isolation or surface-level relationships.

The rules about having friends at work are changing. People start businesses with their friends, they refer their friends into great companies, and they partner with their friends on world-changing work. In Tom Rath's book *Vital Friends: The People You Can't Afford to Live Without*, he reports that employees who have best friends at work are seven times more likely to be engaged in their jobs – and if they have at least three vital friends at work, 96% more likely to be satisfied with their lives![4]

There are two traps high performers often fall victim to when making friends at work:

- **Making everything a competition.** It's tempting to become hyper-competitive with your peers. Letting your ambition and enthusiasm default to competitiveness, instead of channeling it toward camaraderie, is a mistake many ambitious people, myself included, are guilty of. Sure, maybe only one of you will get promoted at the end of this year, but each of you will build impactful, fulfilling careers, and next year the roles may be reversed. Stay in touch, cheer for each other, and remember that the world is smaller than you think.

- **Letting the hierarchy get in the way.** Limiting your potential friendship pool to strictly your same-level peers is self-sabotaging. It's also unlikely to be feasible in the long term; someone is going to change roles eventually. I was working with a leader recently who called his boss one of his best friends. Even as a friendship-at-work champion, I was caught off guard by the open admission of *best friend*, especially at a senior level. He elaborated on their friendship, saying, "Well, I worked for him at this other company. But then through a reorg, he ended up working for me. After that, he got a great opportunity here, so he took it, and eventually asked me to join his team. We worked for each other switching roles on and off for a decade or so, at two different companies."

They stayed friends. No matter who the "boss" was at the time. You can be friends with your boss or the people who report to you, too, provided they're a willing participant and you don't have some archaic HR policy prohibiting it.

You may be thinking: So what happens if you have to fire your friend because the business is underperforming? Well, it sucks. But if you're an empathetic, heart-centered leader . . . firing anyone sucks.

What about if your friend has to give you a not-great performance review? Wouldn't it be better if it came from someone who you knew cared about you, and wanted you to get better?

Can friendship at work make things a little bit messy? Yes. But it also makes work a lot more fun, interesting, and productive. It's an upside that's well worth a moment or two of potential awkwardness.

Don't let leading yourself put blinders on your view of work. Friendship, humor, and camaraderie matter, even if they aren't on your performance review.

Dealing with Lazy Ants

When you read the title of this section, I'm willing to bet a specific person jumped into the forefront of your mind. Most people have a coworker or two who seem to be doing anything besides, well, *working*. Sometimes, their neglected work falls onto your desk, making their entire existence even more frustrating.

It's a common experience: some people do all the heavy lifting while others wander about. This maddening dynamic occurs throughout the entire animal kingdom. Even in ants.

Eisuke Hasegawa, a professor of Agriculture at Hokkaido University, studies lazy ants. According to Hasegawa, at any given moment, half of the ants in the colony are basically doing nothing. They're grooming, aimlessly walking around, or just lying still.

It's easy to assume these colonies aren't efficient, with a significant portion of their population simply meandering through life. Hasegawa's research proves otherwise. In reality, colonies with a significant percentage

All Those Other People

of do-nothing types are actually more resilient. They have a reserve work-force to replace dead or tired worker ants.[5]

What do we take from that? Donna-do-nothing is allowed to slack off, only picking up the slack if you're literally worked to death? That's not ideal.

Over the course of your career, you will encounter your fair share of lazy ants. You likely already have. So, how do you inspire them to wake up early, crush their deliverables, and finally contribute to the meeting?

You don't.

By now, you've hopefully picked up on a running theme in this book: *control the controllable.*

You will not solve this inter-species qualm; lazy ants are an inevitable part of any colony. In high-performing organizations, they're often less frequent (thanks to performance management and good hiring). But one or two will slip through, inevitably.

Here's what you *can* control when it comes to lazy ants:

- **Your own emotional response.** These lazy ants are probably not telling you off in their shower speech or texting their spouse about you. To them, you're likely just another goody-two-shoes worker ant. They know (because you've proven) that you'll do the work. Bringing your frustration, resentment, and righteous indignation into the equation will probably not change their behavior. Accepting an inevitable lazy ant is empowering. It gives you the emotional freedom to stop ruminating and wishing they'd change. They're a part of every species; your office isn't immune.

- **Your requests of them.** The most frustrating part of dealing with a slacker coworker is when they make more work for you. As Hasegawa dove deeper into the underpinning of lazy ants, he reached an important conclusion: The lazy ants *will* respond to a stimulus. If there's a major threat or disruption to the colony, the lazy ants spring into action. So, it turns out that you don't need to die for them to work; you just need to create some urgency.

If you must enlist the help of a lazy ant, dial up the crisis mode. This tactic won't work forever but it can get you through a group project or two. The more you can (truthfully) articulate the impact of the work, and the consequence of the work going un-done, the more likely you are to see a jump in momentum. The lazy ants need to see: *this isn't just business as usual. Something new is happening and people are counting on me.*

- **Your paper trail.** Ants don't get performance reviews. If they did, they'd probably have a harder time embracing their lazy comrades. You, on the other hand, likely do get evaluated on your contributions. Thus, you must protect yourself, and create some distance between you and the lazy ants. The most effective way to do this is with a paper trail. If you have a conversation, send an email recapping the agreed-upon next steps and deadlines. Even if you feel like you're screaming into a void. Even if the thought of typing "just following up on the below!" again makes you want to hide under your desk. Putting *who* is doing *what* by *when* in writing protects you and your contributions should the colony (i.e., project, task force, committee) disintegrate.

When you're leading yourself, you cannot stand to be sabotaged by every lazy ant in your life. A lazy ant does not take away momentum from an ambitious ant. Your slacker coworkers don't have to steal your momentum, either. Just leave them to wander.

Who Is the Common Denominator?

"All my exes are crazy." It's arguably the biggest dating red flag there is. Someone who says that everyone they've dated is crazy is most certainly crazy themselves.

Being aware of your own idiosyncrasies prepares you to deal with the idiosyncrasies of others.

If you're continually frustrated with other people, it's worth noting . . . you're the common denominator in all of those relationships. It's a sobering truth and I say it with love.

Identifying your own triggers, responses that aren't serving you, or relationship patterns you fall into can save you from a lot of frustration.

Here's how it plays out for me: I'm a people pleaser, to a fault. My deepest fear is letting people down. I've been this way my whole life. In first grade, my teacher gave the class a lecture because the substitute the day prior left a note that our class was poorly behaved. I took it so personally. I went home and cried to my mom, so upset that my teacher was disappointed in me. Even though I'm sure I was perfectly behaved (oldest daughter + anxiety, a typical "pleasure to have in class").

People pleasers, and I include myself in that category, tend to take critiques or constructive feedback very personally. That tendency played out in my personal and professional relationships. I perceived a level of blame, shame, or disappointment that wasn't actually present.

Now I know that I have that tendency, and when I feel myself getting triggered, instead of assuming the person giving feedback wants me to cry myself to sleep, I lean into it. I try to be someone who doesn't take feedback so personally.

It could be that you're attracted to chaotic situations or people. Perhaps you're a control freak, continually annoyed that other people are "too relaxed." Maybe you're not enthusiastic about your work and are frustrated by everyone who seems to "care too much."

When you know yourself better, you show up better. Mindset creates behavior. Behavior is the most powerful form of communication. It builds (or destroys) your relationships.

We all leave an emotional wake behind us. The people who work with you are impacted by you. You are the common denominator in all of your relationships and you decide, *how do you want to be known?*

When people say "We have to tell (your name)," do you want them to groan or be excited?

Giving the Benefit of the Doubt (Even to People Who Seemingly Don't Deserve It)

Whenever someone cut my mom off in traffic, she would always look at me and say, "They must be on their way to the hospital." Whether she did this in an effort to instill empathy in me at a young age or just to tamper her own profanity, I have no idea.

Intellectually, we know that everyone is going through something. Emotionally, that's hard to remember in frustrating moments. It's even more difficult when your performance is interconnected with someone who is letting you down or making you frustrated.

This passage from *The Seven Habits of Highly Effective People* changed the way I interact with people who are getting under my skin:[6]

> I remember a mini-paradigm shift I experienced one Sunday morning on a subway in New York. People were sitting quietly – some reading newspapers, some lost in thought, some resting with their eyes closed. It was a calm, peaceful scene.
>
> Then suddenly, a man and his children entered the subway car. The children were so loud and rambunctious that instantly the whole climate changed.
>
> The man sat down next to me and closed his eyes, apparently oblivious to the situation. The children were yelling back and forth, throwing things, even grabbing people's papers. It was very disturbing. And yet, the man sitting next to me did nothing.
>
> It was difficult not to feel irritated. I could not believe that he could be so insensitive as to let his children run wild like that and do nothing about it, taking no responsibility at all. It was easy to see that everyone else on the subway felt irritated, too. So finally, with what I felt like was unusual patience and restraint, I turned to him and said, "Sir, your children are really disturbing a lot of people. I wonder if you couldn't control them a little more?"

The man lifted his gaze as if to come to a consciousness of the situation for the first time and said softly, "Oh, you're right. I guess I should do something about it. We just came from the hospital where their mother died about an hour ago. I don't know what to think, and I guess they don't know how to handle it either."

How would you feel if you told him (or even thought to yourself) that he was a terrible father – and then you found out what happened? You'd probably feel like the world's biggest jerk. That very same dynamic could be playing out with the person you grumble about.

> Giving someone the benefit of the doubt is as much for them as it is for you. Assuming they had a rough childhood, are dealing with a health issue, or just got chewed out by their boss releases you from active anger and moves your mind into a place of tactical maneuvering.

Giving people grace doesn't sentence you to an endless string of "no problem!" when someone misses a deadline and you don't have to take it on the chin every time your boss is a jerk. You manage the situation as best you can, and most importantly, you protect yourself and your work. Set boundaries, leave a paper trail, and hold space for the possibility that things may improve, but accept that they might not.

If you're working with or for this person, you still have to deal with it, but you don't have to carry rage while you work.

Through your career, you'll likely have coworkers who become lifelong friends. You'll also have coworkers that are seemingly attempting to drive you insane. To lead yourself, you must be able to manage both.

REMEMBER

- YOU TEACH PEOPLE HOW TO TREAT YOU. EVEN WHEN YOU'RE NOT FORMALLY IN CHARGE, YOU DEFINE THE EXPERIENCE OF WORKING WITH YOU. SETTING CLEAR EXPECTATIONS IS IMPERATIVE.

- IF YOU PREDICT EXPECTATIONS WILL NOT BE MET, DEFINE CLEAR, INDIVIDUAL RESPONSIBILITIES (KEEPS SOMEONE FROM PASSING BLAME), ADD BUFFER TIME, AND TELL THEM YOU'RE WORRIED.

- BE CAREFUL SPENDING TOO MUCH TIME WITH THE PEOPLE WHO REINFORCE THE NEGATIVITY CYCLE. BE EVEN MORE CAREFUL ABOUT THE ROLE YOU'RE PLAYING. INSTEAD, CHANNEL YOUR ENERGY TO CREATING SUPPORTIVE FRIENDSHIPS.

- IF YOU CONTINUALLY EXPERIENCE THE SAME FRUSTRATING RELATIONSHIP PATTERNS WITH MULTIPLE PEOPLE, LOOK IN THE MIRROR.

Chapter 12

Your Next Play

"Thank you . . . next."

—Ariana Grande

A job change can feel exciting, exhausting, scary, and fulfilling all at the same time. Even a move within your current team comes with challenges and risks.

Traditionally, it was expected that someone would stay with a single company for a long time, regularly climbing a very linear org chart with predictable salary increases each year or two.

Those trajectories still exist, but they're no longer the norm. In 2024, it's estimated that the average person will have 16–17 different jobs in their lifetime, which can translate to about 5–7 career changes.[1]

There are several factors contributing to the shift:

- **Decreasing loyalty (on both sides).** Millennials watched their parents get fired in 2008, after investing decades with a single employer. The news is filled with organizations paying unfair wages, maintaining discriminatory policies, and demonstrating a general lack of empathy. I currently know *one* person with a pension, and they're 79. Many organizations renounced historical loyalty to their employees, and unsurprisingly, employees returned the favor.

- **Careers (and lives) are getting longer.** Many Americans are working into their 70s and 80s – or longer – because of longer life spans, changing attitudes about retirement, and insufficient savings. The average person will work 90,000 hours over the course of their life. It's not surprising there's a growing need for some variety.

- **Technology is changing at an exponential rate.** As artificial intelligence and machine learning develop, new occupations and even new industries are arising. This technological leap is also causing the elimination or consolidation of jobs that are readily mechanized. Opportunities look different now than 10 years ago, and in 10 years, they'll be different from today.

The world is changing. Your career changing is inevitable, even if you technically stay in the same job.

To lead yourself, you'll need to be intentional about defining and creating the career you want. Yet, you're only part of the equation. Your plans likely depend on other people. You'll need to navigate when things don't go according to your plan, identify a good opportunity (even if you weren't looking), and spot red flags before it's too late. That's where your "next play" comes in.

Don't Linger Too Long

"Next play" is phraseology I first heard at LinkedIn. In the last decade, I've seen how LinkedIn commits to the growth and development of their employees in a way very few other organizations do.

In an interview, LinkedIn Executive Chairman and former CEO Jeff Weiner shares how he came to the "next play" philosophy, originally termed by legendary Duke Blue Devils coach Mike Krzyzewski.

"Every time the basketball team goes up and down the court and they complete a sequence, offense or defense, Coach K yells out the exact same thing, every time. He yells out 'next play!' because he doesn't want the team lingering too long on what just took place," Weiner said in an interview with *The New York Times*.

That goes for successes as well as failures, he explained. "You can take a moment to reflect on what just happened, and you probably should, but you shouldn't linger too long on it, and then move on to the next play."[2]

I've seen firsthand how teammates at LinkedIn think and talk about their "next play" when planning their careers. Contemplating a career change isn't an internal crisis; it's an open conversation with their colleagues. Looking for a new job isn't an anxiety-inducing secret. It's a process, one often supported by their manager, even if that new job isn't at LinkedIn.

I asked Jolie Miller (a Director at LinkedIn, who I referenced in Chapter 1) to explain her personal thinking behind "next play." Here's what she said: "At the end of the day, companies come and go, but relationships, and caring about someone as a person means a lot to me as a people leader. If it's time to move on from your current role, internally or externally, and we can open a door, we will."

Your boss may not have the intentional, generous spirit that Jolie and so many leaders at LinkedIn have. That shouldn't stop you from crafting your next play, even if it's not a move you make this year.

While there's some compelling research around increasing your earnings via regular job changes, if you're happy, you don't need to change jobs to find increasing fulfillment. Staying put, for now, might be a perfectly viable choice. Unfortunately, it's a "choice" many make reactively, based on fear.

There's no shortage of support in just keeping things as they are. You've undoubtedly heard things like "The grass isn't always greener!" or "The beast you know is better than the beast you don't!" and even "Bird in the hand is worth two in the bush" when talking about potential moves. Unless your job (or boss) is truly awful, odds are, no one will actively push you to change.

It takes a lot of courage to do something different. After getting degrees, investing time to learn, building relationships, and growing in your role, a change can feel like you're giving up a lot of work you did. You're not.

> You don't have to live your entire life in the service of the college major you picked when you were 19.

In *Range: Why Generalists Triumph in a Specialized World*, David Epstein studied the early backgrounds of high performers. His takeaways reinforce that a windy path is often the most effective.

Here's what he found:

> Eventual elites typically devote less time early on to deliberate practice in the activity in which they will eventually become experts. Instead, they undergo what researchers call a "sampling period." They play a variety of sports, usually in an unstructured or lightly structured environment; they gain a range of physical proficiencies from which they can draw; they learn about their own abilities and proclivities; and only later do they focus in and ramp up technical practice in one area.[3]

A diversity of career experiences increases the likelihood of success and satisfaction. Leading yourself doesn't sentence you to a perfectly linear career path. It does the opposite. When you have the mindset to navigate change, find meaning in the mundane, and control the controllable, potential opportunities become more expansive.

You don't need to make a move this year. You might not even make one in the next decade. Still, your next play should be a lens you look at your career through, because living the current play for the rest of your life is most definitely selling yourself short.

Honing in on Your Superpower

People who use their strengths every day are six times more likely to be engaged on the job.[4] Knowing your superpower enables you to define a career path that you uniquely are more likely to enjoy and succeed in.

If the suggestion that you have a superpower feels awkward, it's probably for one of these reasons:

- You (wrongfully) assume that because your superpower comes easy for you, it comes easy for everyone, and therefore, it's not a superpower.

- Your superpower has been discounted and deemed unimportant in previous endeavors.

- You're hyper-competitive and believe that because you are not the single best in the world at whatever your superpower is, it's not your superpower.

A helpful way to uncover or get reacquainted with your superpower is to put the function of your job aside. I say that because no one's "superpower" is being a product manager. Nor is it being a data analyst, a paralegal, or a consultant. Examining your gifts only through the lens of your current position is going to make you miss something.

Your superpower isn't your job, but it is likely what enables you to be good at your job. For example, good recruiters have an innate ability to read people. Project managers tend to be extremely organized. IT strategists are natural problem solvers.

Viewing prospective opportunities through the lens of your superpower enables you to open your mind to functions or industries that are different than your current reality. Instead of jumping from your company to a competitor, or taking the "senior" version of your current "junior" role, your lens on opportunity becomes wider.

Strip away the details of specific tasks and look more into *how* you do the task. Notice your strengths, what gives you energy, and pay attention to what the people around you are saying.

Mentors can be an exceptional resource in career planning because they generally aren't deep in the weeds of your function. They don't have a vested interest in your next performance review, the strategic plan of next year, or any of the financials.

If the only person you seek career counsel from is your boss, odds are, you'll end up exactly like your boss. That might not be a bad thing if you have a great boss. Still, a diversity of perspectives is paramount.

Over-indexing on the advice of a single mentor in career planning results in a couple of challenges:

- **Your mentor is biased.** They may be partial to believing you should stay with your company because they want to work with you. They may think you should follow a particular path because that's what they did and it worked.

- **They don't see the whole picture.** I'm sure you don't share every detail of your psyche with your mentors. They're offering (well-intended) advice with limited information.

You can do whatever you want with your career. It's a petrifying yet freeing realization. You might not be able to 180 your work life tomorrow, but you can set the wheels in motion any time you choose to.

Networking (Ugh)

Networking events give me the ick. They're full of pushy salespeople, the food is bad, and the conversations are generally awkward. Yet you know, to execute your next play, you're going to need the help of someone else.

You don't have to sign up for an industry meet-up if you don't want to. In fact, you're probably doing more networking *inside* of your company than you realize. The in-the-cadence-of-business working relationships that you've built count.

Here's some advice I got from Jolie, about making your networking game even stronger:

> Seek out sponsors. Find people who are higher up, who you can get to know, who will bring up your name in rooms you're not in, when talking about strategy, and in annual review calibrations. Ally relationships are powerful; you want a network of people who are rooting for you.

You don't have to wait for a senior leader to tap you on the shoulder and dub you the "chosen one" for future growth opportunities. Jolie suggests, "You can start this process yourself, by saying, 'Hey, (VP), I would love to help you with this thing I heard you talk about in the all hands. If there's any way I can be useful, let me know.'"

If a cold outreach to a senior leader gives you the heebie-jeebies, take the pressure off yourself. Instead of focusing on forging new relationships, dial into the relationships you've already built. Solidifying these touchpoints matter, even if it's decades down the road.

Here's some counsel on networking from Dorie Clark, the author of *The Long Game: How to Be a Long-Term Thinker in a Short-Term World:*

> Over time, the value of long-term professional connections, even extremely light and extremely casual ones magnifies. There's a concept in sociology called dormant ties. There's a reputational value and a comfort level people have with you because they've known you for a long time, even if you haven't talked in years, and even if they don't know you well. As a result of that, it becomes a lot easier to do business, get business, and get referrals as you get older, because you know so many people that have been peripherally aware of you for a long time.

Ideally, networking doesn't feel like "networking." You've seen through this book how leading yourself is dependent upon knowing what gives you energy, fuels your spirit, and propels your momentum. If awkward networking events are going to leave you drained, don't go.

Widen your lens to what relationship building can mean. Raising your hand internally, making the first outreach, and keeping up with your colleagues *is* networking. These relationships, even if they don't seem like anything more than a casual familiarity now, will add up to make a substantial positive impact on your career.

There are exceptions, though . . .

Don't Burn Bridges . . . Except in These Three Situations

We've all had moments where we force ourselves to bite our tongue. Maybe it's an erratic boss, a less-than-tactful coworker, or a downright rude customer. At the moment, you sit there calmly, with the age-old adage in the back of your mind: *don't burn your bridges.*

This long-time career advice is well intended; any seasoned professional will tell you that the world is smaller than you think. But when taken to an extreme, this advice can leave people feeling powerless in futile, toxic, and even abusive situations. Leading yourself means *you* own *your* next step. You can move forward despite burning the bridge behind you, especially in these three situations.

The Person (or Company) Has a Terrible Reputation

During college, I worked for a small business. The owner was awful. He had bad relationships with his vendors, frequent emotional outbursts, and to top it off, our checks were always late. Anyone you asked would describe him as a misogynistic jerk.

I eventually quit, saying I was leaving for a "better opportunity" (in truth, I didn't have another job lined up). I stuck out my several weeks of notice, despite a plethora of passive-aggressive remarks from a grown man.

Here's what I wish I knew then: If you experience someone as consistently terrible, you're probably not the only one. Everyone has a reputation, and a reference from someone with an awful one isn't as helpful to you as you think.

You Already Tried (Many Times) to Be Diplomatic

Fool me once, shame on you, fool me twice shame on me. I err on the side of giving people the benefit of the doubt, and I confess I often let people have too many chances. What I've painfully learned over time, is chances 7, or 8, or 9 . . . usually aren't any different.

Everyone has bad days and makes mistakes, and you certainly don't want to write someone off too quickly. Yet, when someone shows you who they are (consistently), believe them. (Thank you, Maya Angelou.)

There's Something Undeniably Weird Going On

If there's something illegal, immoral, or just really fishy going on, don't look the other way. These things very rarely get less suspicious over time. You don't want to attach your reputation to a leader, or organization, that is (or soon to be) unethical.

I recently binge-watched *The Dropout*, on Hulu. It's the miniseries that tells the story of Elizabeth Holmes, the founder of Theranos. Here's the short of it: Theranos was an organization that went from a perceived "breakthrough medical technology company" to being recognized as a giant scam. Holmes, the founder, was recently found guilty of conspiracy and fraud. The entire company, several hundred people, was built on the lies of a few people at the top. But it took years for those lies to be exposed publicly. The high-profile scandal broke long after things started feeling weird inside of the company.

The whistleblowers in that situation (Tyler Shultz, Adam Rosendorff, and Erika Cheung, most notably) will have a lasting reputation as upstanding, honorable people. The slew of scientists, salespeople, and mid-level leaders who knowingly chose to turn a blind eye . . . not so much.

Don't compromise yourself to save face in a situation that doesn't deserve it. If a bridge will do nothing but lead you back to an ever-lasting steaming pile of garbage, why not burn it?

When It Doesn't Go According to Plan

Did your career go exactly according to plan? Are you doing exactly what you thought you could be when you first set out on this journey? Probably not. Few people are.

Part of leading yourself is being able to pivot when things don't go according to plan.

Here was my plan at age 22: Get promoted to senior account manager at an ad agency by 25. Then director by 30. Then VP by 35. Then COO by 40. None of that happened, and looking back, I'm glad it didn't play out like that.

Intellectually, you know your career won't go according to plan 100% of the time. Emotionally, derailments from a well-defined plan can feel like a major setback.

Plan derailments generally fall into one of three buckets:

- **Interview disappointments.** You muster the courage to put yourself out there and interview for a new job. After three interviews, two case studies, and an escape room, it turns out the hiring manager's nephew is a "better fit." So fun! Interviewing is a vulnerable experience. You have to openly admit that you want something while the decision of whether or not you get it is in someone else's hands. Being passed over hurts and can quickly kill your enthusiasm if you sit in the hurt for too long.

- **Layoffs.** Sometimes your next play is forced on you, like if you get fired, or more commonly, laid off. It's common for organizations to pin this on some outside force, so your leader doesn't become "the bad guy." In the book *The Firm: The Story of McKinsey and Its Secret Influence on American Business*, mega consulting firm McKinsey was described as "without question the go-to consultants for managers seeking justification for savage cost-cutting as well as a convenient scapegoat on who to blame it."[5] No matter how many times you hear "don't take it personally" or "it was a business decision," a layoff or firing is generally a long-lasting emotional sting.

- **A logistics curveball.** The job you wanted was remote, and now it's in the office. You thought you could handle working 50 hours a week, and life said otherwise. Your spouse got a great opportunity, and now you have to change the course. The universe threw you a curveball and now, the plan you had in mind just isn't feasible.

Whether it's a hiring manager, a CEO, or some logistical constraint in the universe saying *no* to the plan you had in mind, a plan derailment is rarely welcomed. The only thing you can do at this point is believe there is something better for you out there. Trust that this part of your journey will count for something.

You have nothing to lose by clinging to optimism and everything to gain.

When It *Does* Go According to Plan . . . and Still Feels Bad

Actually getting what you worked so hard for rarely lives up to the expectations that fueled your efforts.

Last year I was talking to a friend who teaches an undergraduate course at Harvard. He shared an interesting phenomenon: When someone is accepted into Harvard, they're typically at the top of their class. Compared to their high school peers, they had better grades, more extracurriculars, and higher scores on the SAT.

Then . . . they arrive at Harvard. Suddenly, they're not the smartest student in class anymore. Everyone has the same (or better) achievements as they do. Overnight, they go from being a standout to being one of the indistinguishable masses, blending in just like every other member of the freshman class.

The same thing happens at work. When you make it to the top of your field – whether that's getting a job at the top firm, being awarded a certain distinction, or making it to the C-Suite – you go from a star player to just another member of the team. The praise, recognition, and achievement you got used to as a top performer is in short supply at the top *because everyone you're with did the same thing as you.* That's why they're there.

The new reality is almost always, in some way, disappointing. It could be because you're like the Harvard freshman, no longer special. It could be because your new boss, your new projects, and your new team aren't as interesting as you hoped for. It could be because you did in fact make the wrong call.

Unless you're leaving a toxic work environment, you'll likely experience some awkward growing pains that can send a surge of doubt through your brain.

Take a breather before you jump to conclusions. Is your new team as friendly as your old one? Of course not, you just met them. Do you feel like you're not as good at your new job as you were at your previous one? Of course you do. Emphasis on the word "new." Is your new boss hard to understand? Obviously. You're still getting to know them.

If time marches on and the thought that you made the wrong choice is only getting louder, you must act. Clinging to the wrong job because you don't want to admit it's the wrong job will cost you too much energy, time, and career momentum. You're not the first person to take a misstep.

Remember, a 2023 *Harvard Business Review* report showed 28% of new hires in a multi-year study were boomerang hires (employees who had resigned within the previous 36 months).[6]

It's better to admit you walked through the wrong door than spend your whole life in the wrong room.

The time you've already spent interviewing, onboarding, and trying to make it work are sunk costs. You made a play, it didn't work out how you thought it would, and you learned. What's the next play?

Listening to Your Gut When Your Gut Has Anxiety

Career planning is never clear-cut, no matter how many articles on LinkedIn suggest it is. No one can address *your* nuance besides *you*. Even the most informed, smart, experienced person will not have the all-encompassing view of your life that you have.

I have anxiety. My gut isn't always right. She's kind of a worst-case scenario gal, if left unchecked. There have to be some parameters beyond blindly listening to gnawing feelings. Those feelings are valid, but they're often not the entire picture.

That's why so many people fall back on the saying "trust your gut." It makes sense in theory. Our subconscious can pick up on emotional undercurrents, possible outcomes, and other nuances the conscious part of our mind misses. The brain is an incredible thing and human intuition is nothing short of magic.

"Trust your gut" is well-intended advice, but it puts a lot of pressure on the accuracy of your intuition during a time of stress.

If you're on the brink of making your next play, and feeling anxious about it, reflecting on three prompts can help:

- **"What if it goes awesome?"** We talked about this one in Chapter 3. You've undoubtedly spent hours contemplating the risk. Indulge your mind to consider an optimistic alternative, at least for a minute.

- **"What would I do if I wasn't afraid?"** You don't have to actually do it, just think about it. The prompt reveals what's deep in your heart, beneath your anxiety.

- **"What's the worst that happens?"** When you actually spell out the worst-case scenario (the job doesn't work out, you don't like it, you come crying back to your current employer, whatever it is), you may find it's not as scary as the pit in your stomach would lead you to believe. Odds are, no one is going to shoot you or put up a billboard with your face on it that says "idiot." Pinpointing what you're afraid of, instead of sitting in the feeling of "general fear," enables you to be more objective.

Your mind is a powerful thing, but it takes some direction to serve you in the way you need it to. Just like you've learned to be intentional with behavior and relationships, be intentional with your thoughts. Here's a metaphor that may give you the final push you need-

It's often said that elephant handlers will train a baby elephant to be submissive by chaining them to a stake in the ground when they're young. The baby elephant tries to break free day after day and eventually gives up because it's too weak. The elephant grows, years pass, and the elephant remains chained to the stake. But at this point, the elephant weighs thousands of pounds. It's more than capable of ripping the stake out of the ground with little effort.

Yet, the grown elephant never attempts, because it believes the stake in the ground is too strong. After some reflection, you may come to realize that the only thing holding you back from your next play is your own fears, beliefs, and anxiety.

Leading yourself doesn't guarantee you'll make each move with 100% confidence, and it doesn't mean you'll make the right move every time. It means that despite being afraid, despite some ambiguity or unrest, you make a play.

REMEMBER

- CAREER CHANGES ARE INEVITABLE, WHETHER THEY HAPPEN TO YOU OR YOU MAKE THEM HAPPEN. PUT YOURSELF IN THE DRIVER'S SEAT BY ALWAYS THINKING ABOUT YOUR NEXT PLAY, EVEN IF YOU'RE NOT PLANNING TO MAKE A MOVE SOON.

- HONE IN ON YOUR SUPERPOWERS, WHAT GIVES YOU ENERGY, AND WHAT YOU'RE BEST AT BY STRIPPING AWAY THE FUNCTIONALITY OF YOUR JOB AND FOCUSING MORE ON THE "HOW."

- A STRONG NETWORK, INSIDE AND OUTSIDE OF YOUR COMPANY, IS CRUCIAL FOR MAKING YOUR NEXT PLAY.

- YOU CAN BURN BRIDGES, CHANGE YOUR MIND, GET LAID OFF, AND STILL MOVE FORWARD. CAREERS AREN'T A ONE-TIME DECISION; THEY'RE A PROCESS.

Conclusion

L eading yourself is a conscious choice to own your power, even when the industry, your boss, or rapidly changing technology makes you feel powerless.

Identifying what you *can* control is the antidote to burnout. Recognizing that you're in charge of you is what gives you the emotional freedom to create the career you want. It's what gives you the authority to create the *life* you want.

I've facilitated the journey from a "disempowered corporate underling" to "fully alive self-starter" with thousands of people in my decade of corporate work. I've also made (well, am making) that journey myself.

It doesn't require a job change, a boss change, or a massive career upheaval. With the same job and the same boss, a different work experience is possible.

I frequently observe, star players are not usually the best coaches. The best coaches are the middle-of-the-pack players, who worked hard and got pretty good. For the star player, things come more naturally. Yes, they worked at it. But they also got lucky, being born with an innate skillset. The middle-tier player had to learn. They had to break it down, fight uphill, and push harder, just to be pretty good. When it comes to leading yourself, I was the middle-of-the-pack player who had to learn. I became a good coach because I've lived in the struggle.

My own motivation has waxed and waned throughout my career. I've battled imposter syndrome, burnout, boredom, isolation, and every other angst that's part of the work experience. My inner emo-kid still makes an appearance every once in a while. I don't execute the concepts in this book perfectly, even though I wrote it. I strive for 80%. That's enough.

When I first contracted for this book, I was deep in the throes of post-partum depression. I had lost my sense of agency. I cried on the bathroom floor, all the time, wondering if I would ever regain control of my life. For the first time I could remember, I felt totally powerless. Motherhood rocked me. For you, that powerless feeling may have come from somewhere else in your life.

We are who we are, at work and at home. Our ability to lead ourselves transcends the space we're operating in. Whether you're up against a sleepless infant, a boss who is a jerk, a struggling industry, or overly ambitious targets, how you show up for *yourself* is the biggest indicator of your success.

Some circumstances are devastatingly awful. Way worse than a colicky baby. I'd like to think the first six months of motherhood will be the most challenging period of my life, but I know that probably won't be the case.

For months, I didn't share the depth of my pain with anyone. I was scared and ashamed of my own thoughts. I stuffed every ounce of struggle so deep, that on the surface, I looked like I was thriving.

That's another (unfortunate) commonality among self-starters . . . *They wear it well.*

They take on another project, despite barely treading water. They always pick up the slack when their team drops the ball. They serve on the committee, mentor the new hire, rework the presentation deck, and they're always available to proof an email. Some even sign a book deal when they're emotionally spiraling. 😉 And often, nobody suspects a thing.

The practices in this book work. Mindfulness, intentionality, and self-leadership have the power to change your life. But sometimes they're not enough. Therapy, medication, and professional help are tools for high achievers, too. It's OK if you can't independently brain-hack your way to being OK.

I've talked in this book about seizing opportunity, taking calculated risks, and forging your own path, even if you're doing it alone. You can't do that when you're run ragged. To lead yourself, you must take care of yourself.

Writing this book has been a cathartic self-reclamation. Through hundreds of conversations and copious research, I've witnessed the power of mindset, intention, and thoughtful relationships. With practice, I started to re-experience that power myself.

I hope you see that you, too, can lead yourself to something greater. Even if the feeling of inspiration is a blurry memory or if the fully engaged version of *you* seems far away.

Your family, your friends, and even your workplace deserve you at your best. More importantly than that, you deserve to be at your best. You deserve to feel like your life is purposeful, joyful, and full of opportunity . . . *because it is.*

Notes

Introduction

1. Liu, A. (2019). Making joy a priority at work. *Harvard Business Review* (17 July). https://hbr.org/2019/07/making-joy-a-priority-at-work (accessed 10 April 2024).
2. Wells, R. (2023). 5 easy ways to spot career and job growth opportunities. *Forbes* (15 November). http://www.forbes.com/sites/rachelwells/2023/11/15/5-easy-ways-to-spot-career-and-job-growth-opportunities (accessed 10 April 2024).
3. Brady, S. (2022). 82% of workers would consider quitting their jobs because of a bad manager. ValuePenguin. http://www.valuepenguin.com/news/majority-workers-would-leave-job-becuase-of-manager (accessed 10 April 2024).
4. Davidson, P. (2023). Is a recession coming? Or will it be a soft landing? Pay attention to these market signals. *USA Today* (14 August). http://www.usatoday.com/story/money/2023/08/10/recession-or-soft-landing-2023/70555621007 (accessed 10 April 2024).
5. Smith, M. (2022). New survey says these are the 3 most annoying co-worker habits—here's how to handle them. CNBC. http://www.cnbc.com/2022/03/19/new-survey-says-these-are-the-3-most-annoying-co-worker-habits.html (accessed 10 April 2024).
6. Wills, B. (2023). Does your workforce spend too much time searching for information?. ProProfs. http://www.proprofskb.com/blog/workforce-spend-much-time-searching-information/#:~:text=According%20to%20a%20McKinsey%20report,but%20not%20contributing%20any%20value! (accessed 10 April 2024).
7. Haaland, M. (2024). The top tech issues that make employed americans switch jobs. SWNS Digital. https://swnsdigital.com/us/2022/11/the-top-tech-issues-that-make-employed-americans-switch-jobs (accessed 4 January 2024).
8. Laker, B. (2021). 94% of workers are stressed: KPMG research reveals Covid-19's lingering effects on employees. *Forbes* (4 May). http://www.forbes.com/sites/benjaminlaker/2021/05/04/the-future-world-of-work-is-fascinating-reveals-new-research-from-kpmg (accessed 10 April 2024).

Chapter 1

1. Klotz, A., Derler, A., Kim, C., and Winlaw, M. (2023). The promise (and risk) of boomerang employees. *Harvard Business Review* (15 March). https://hbr .org/2023/03/the-promise-and-risk-of-boomerang-employees (accessed 10 April 2024).

2. Locapo, D. (2022). 15+ million pandemic-era U.S. job quitters say they were better off in their old job. UKG. http://www.ukg.com/about-us/newsroom/ 15-million-pandemic-era-us-job-quitters-say-they-were-better-their-old-job (accessed 10 April 2024).

3. Adkins, A. (2015). U.S. employee engagement reaches three-year high. Gallup. https://news.gallup.com/poll/181895/employee-engagement-reaches-three-year-high.aspx (accessed 10 April 2024).

4. Gallup. Employee engagement. http://www.gallup.com/394373/indicator-employee-engagement.aspx (accessed 4 January 2024).

5. University of Notre Dame. Aristotle's nicomachean ethics: Learn to live well. https://philife.nd.edu/aristotle-s-nicomachean-ethics-learn-to-live-well (accessed 4 January 2024).

6. Hansen, M. (2019). *Great at Work: The Hidden Habits of Top Performers*. Simon & Schuster.

7. Behl, M. (2019). How Japanese concepts of IKIGAI, mindfulness can make our lives wholesome and rewarding. Firstpost. http://www.firstpost.com/ tech/science/how-japanese-concepts-of-ikigai-mindfulness-can-make-our-lives-wholesome-and-rewarding-7370861.html (accessed 10 April 2024).

8. WorldOMeter. Life expectancy of the world population. https://www .worldometers.info/demographics/life-expectancy (accessed 10 April 2024).

9. Alimujiang, A., Wiensch, A., Boss, J. et al. (2019). Association between life purpose and mortality among US adults older than 50 years. *JAMA Network*. https:// doi.org/10.1001/jamanetworkopen.2019.4270 (accessed 4 January 2024).

10. Grant, A. (2010). Putting a face to a name: The art of motivating employees. Wharton. U Penn. https://knowledge.wharton.upenn.edu/article/putting-a-face-to-a-name-the-art-of-motivating-employees (accessed 10 April 2024).

11. Good, V. (2018). Motivating salespeople toward greater productivity. Michigan State University. http://www.proquest.com/docview/2293039647 (accessed 10 April 2024).

12. Achor, S., Reece, A., Kellerman, G.R., and Robichaux, A. (2018). 9 out of 10 people are willing to earn less money to do more-meaningful work. *Harvard Business Review* (6 November). https://hbr.org/2018/11/9-out-of-10-people-are-willing-to-earn-less-money-to-do-more-meaningful-work (accessed 10 April 2024).

13. Americas EY (2021). Is your purpose lectured, or lived? EY. http://www.ey.com/en_us/purpose/is-your-purpose-lectured-or-lived (accessed 10 April 2024).

14. Terkel, S. (1997). *Working: People Talk About What They Do All Day and How They Feel About What They Do*. The New Press.

15. PWC (2018). Making work more meaningful. PWC|CECP|Imperative. https://cecp.co/wp-content/uploads/2018/12/pwc-building-a-fulfilling-employee-experience.pdf?redirect=no (accessed 10 April 2024).

Chapter 2

1. Frequency illusion. (2024). Wikipedia. https://en.wikipedia.org/wiki/Frequency_illusion (accessed 10 April 2024).

2. Statista Research Department (2023). Civilian labor force in the United States from 1990 to 2022. http://www.statista.com/statistics/191750/civilian-labor-force-in-the-us-since-1990 (accessed 10 April 2024).

3. Constantz, J. (2022). "No one wants to work anymore" is a complaint as old as work itself. Bloomberg. http://www.bloomberg.com/news/articles/2022-08-10/no-one-wants-to-work-anymore-meme-shows-complaint-is-as-old-as-work-itself (accessed 10 April 2024).

4. Kessler, S. (2017). Gen X was as entitled and unmanageable as millennials are, based on commentary of the '90s. QZ. https://qz.com/work/1070139/millennials-are-no-harder-to-manage-than-generation-x-according-to-the-commentary-of-the-1990s (accessed 10 April 2024).

5. Barber, S.. (2015). Socrates on today's youth. Teach with Class. https://susangbarber.com/2015/11/12/socrates-on-todays-youth (accessed 10 April 2024).

6. Durocher, L. (2023). Wikipedia. https://en.wikipedia.org/wiki/Leo_Durocher (accessed 10 April 2024).

7. Vedantam, S. (2017). Instead of showing off wealth, some show off busy schedules. NPR. http://www.npr.org/2017/04/27/525833226/instead-of-showing-off-wealth-some-show-off-busy-schedules (accessed 10 April 2024).

8. Achor, S. and Gielan, M. (2016). The data-driven case for vacation. *Harvard Business Review* (13 July). https://hbr.org/2016/07/the-data-driven-case-for-vacation (accessed 10 April 2024).

9. Groysberg, B. and Abrahams, R. (2020). The Stockdale paradox and survival psychology contain wisdom for how leaders can manage the coronavirus crisis. *Harvard Business School* (17 August). https://hbswk.hbs.edu/item/what-the-stockdale-paradox-tells-us-about-crisis-leadership (accessed 10 April 2024).

10. Bogan, S. (2016). Silence those voices in your head. *Investment News* (30 November). http://www.investmentnews.com/practice-management/opinion/the-limitless-advisor/silence-those-voices-in-your-head-69986 (accessed 10 April 2024).

Chapter 3

1. De Becker, G. (1997). *The Gift of Fear*, 1e. Little, Brown and Company.

Chapter 4

1. Worthy, C. (2020). LinkedIn learning. http://www.linkedin.com/learning/using-emotions-to-leverage-and-accelerate-change-a-guide-for-leaders/what-we-have-been-getting-wrong-about-leading-through-change?autoplay=true&trk=learning-course_tocItem&upsellOrderOrigin=default_guest_learning (accessed 10 April 2024).
2. Jones, D. (2022). Shocking study shows cost of being interrupted at work. tl;dv. https://tldv.io/blog/interruptions-at-work-statistics (accessed 10 April 2024).

Chapter 5

1. Guillebeau, C. (2019). The four burners theory – your thoughts?. The Art of Non-Conformity. https://chrisguillebeau.com/the-four-burners-theory (accessed 10 April 2024).
2. Gallup. Strengths development & coaching. http://www.gallup.com/learning/248405/strengths-development-coaching.aspx (accessed 8 January 2024).
3. Brower, T. (2021). Learning is a sure path to happiness: Science proves it. *Forbes* (17 October). http://www.forbes.com/sites/tracybrower/2021/10/17/learning-is-a-sure-path-to-happiness-science-proves-it/?sh=48b680a6768e (accessed 10 April 2024).
4. Gotian, R. (2022). *The Success Factor: Developing the Mindset and Skillset for Peak Business Performance*. Kogan Page.
5. Stauffer, R. (2023). *All the Gold Stars: Reimagining Ambition and the Ways We Strive*. Hachette Go.

Chapter 6

1. LinkedIn (2018) workplace learning report. https://learning.linkedin.com/resources/workplace-learning-report-2018 (accessed 10 April 2024).

Chapter 7

1. Iacocca, L. (2007). *Iacocca: An Autobiography*. Random House Publishing Group.
2. Brower, T. (2021). Learning is a sure path to happiness: Science proves it. *Forbes* (17 October). http://www.forbes.com/sites/tracybrower/2021/10/17/learning-is-a-sure-path-to-happiness-science-proves-it/?sh=48b680a6768e (accessed 10 April 2024).
3. Stauffer, R. (2023). *All the Gold Stars: Reimagining Ambition and the Ways We Strive*. Hachette Go.

Chapter 8

1. Lotardo, E. and McLeod, L. (2023). How to be a purpose-driven leader without burning out. *Harvard Business Review* (26 July). https://hbr.org/2023/07/how-to-be-a-purpose-driven-leader-without-burning-out (accessed 10 April 2024).
2. Acharya, A., Lieber, R., Seem, L., and Welchman, T. (2017). How to identify the right "Spans of Control" for your organization. McKinsey & Company. http://www.mckinsey.com/capabilities/people-and-organizational-performance/our-insights/how-to-identify-the-right-spans-of-control-for-your-organization (accessed 10 April 2024).
3. Klinghoffer, D. and Kirkpatrick-Husk, K. (2023). More than 50% of managers feel burned out. *Harvard Business Review* (18 May). https://hbr.org/2023/05/more-than-50-of-managers-feel-burned-out (accessed 10 April 2024).
4. Dodgson, L. (2023). A career influencer says millennials and gen Z don't want to be managers anymore – here's why. *Business Insider* (7 November). http://www.businessinsider.com/why-millennials-and-gen-z-dont-want-to-be-managers-2023-11 (accessed 10 April 2024).

Chapter 9

1. McKinsey & Company (2019). Decision making in the age of urgency. http://www.mckinsey.com/capabilities/people-and-organizational-performance/our-insights/decision-making-in-the-age-of-urgency (accessed 10 April 2024).

2. Amazon (2024). Leadership principles. http://www.amazon.jobs/content/en/our-workplace/leadership-principles (accessed 12 January 2024).

Chapter 10

1. Block, M. (2014). What's with all of the "Hairy Arms" in graphic design? *NPR* (17 November). http://www.npr.org/2014/11/17/364760847/whats-with-all-of-the-hairy-arms-in-graphic-design (accessed 10 April 2024).
2. Cohen, S. (2023). 3 Things entrepreneurs should know about advice. *TEDx* (1 August). http://www.youtube.com/watch?v=sVDgOLLL66o (accessed 10 April 2024).

Chapter 11

1. Sklar, D. (2023). Parents warned ahead of July 4 parties that drowning is leading killer of young children. *Times of San Diego* (3 July). https://timesofsandiego.com/crime/2023/07/03/ndpa-reminds-parents-how-fast-and-silent-drowning-can-occur-ahead-of-july-4th-celebrations (accessed 10 April 2024).
2. Bourg Carter, S. (2012). Emotions are contagious – choose your company wisely. *Psychology Today* (20 October). http://www.psychologytoday.com/us/blog/high-octane-women/201210/emotions-are-contagious-choose-your-company-wisely (accessed 10 April 2024).
3. Brown, B. (2017). *Braving the Wilderness: The Quest for True Belonging and the Courage to Stand Alone*. Random House.
4. Rath, T. (2006). *Vital Friends: The People You Can't Afford to Live Without*. Gallup Press.
5. Noguchi, Y. (2016). Before you judge lazy workers, consider they might serve a purpose. *WBUR* (28 March). http://www.wbur.org/npr/468138647/before-you-judge-lazy-workers-consider-they-might-serve-a-purpose (accessed 10 April 2024).
6. Covey, S. (2004). *The 7 Habits of Highly Effective People*. Franklin Covey.

Chapter 12

1. The University of Queensland (2023). How many career changes in a lifetime? https://study.uq.edu.au/stories/how-many-career-changes-lifetime (accessed 10 April 2024).

2. Zetlin, M. (2018). LinkedIn CEO Jeff Weiner says this 2-word sentence will help you achieve long-term success. *Inc.* http://www.inc.com/minda-zetlin/linkedin-ceo-jeff-weiner-mike-krzyzewski-coach-k-next-play-consistent-success.html (accessed 10 April 2024).

3. Epstein, D. (2019). *Range: Why Generalists Triumph in a Specialized World.* Riverhead Books.

4. Sorenson, S. (2024). How employees' strengths make your company stronger. Gallup. https://news.gallup.com/businessjournal/167462/employees-strengths-company-stronger.aspx (accessed 10 January 2024).

5. McDonald, D. (2014). *The Firm: The Story of McKinsey and Its Secret Influence on American Business.* Simon & Schuster.

6. Klotz, A., Derler, A., Kim, C., and Winlaw, M. (2023). The promise (and risk) of boomerang employees. *Harvard Business Review* (15 March). https://hbr.org/2023/03/the-promise-and-risk-of-boomerang-employees (accessed 10 April 2024).

Acknowledgments

Firstly, I'd like to thank my mom and business partner, Lisa McLeod. Your willingness to work through messy ideas, your belief that the world of work can be a force for good, and your unwavering all-in attitude have profoundly shaped this book and who I am as a person.

I'd also like to thank our clients who have, sometimes unknowingly, fueled my belief in the power of self-leadership.

I'm grateful for the team at Wiley: Zach, Amanda, Sangeetha, Georgette, and their colleagues, who believe in the world-changing power of sharing ideas and worked with me to better shape and share my own.

Thank you to the creators and researchers I've cited in this book, particularly Alex Liu, Morten Hansen, Adam Grant, Paul Fairie, Jim Collins, Gavin De Becker, Scott Barry Kaufman, Laura Gassner Otting, Cassandra Worthy, Tessa Romero, David Sedaris, Ruth Gotian, Rainesford Stauffer, Susan Cohen, Brenda Fridman, Brené Brown, Tom Rath, Eisuke Hasegawa, Stephen Covey, Jeff Weiner, and David Epstein.

I'm especially grateful for a few trusted friends and mentors who shared their insights and allowed me to tell their stories in this book: Jolie Miller, Craig Sender, David Cohen, and Dorie Clark.

A huge force behind this book is LinkedIn Learning. LinkedIn Learning has changed the career trajectory of so many learners. It's also changed my own. The people there, the work they put in, and the feedback they give have formed who I am as an instructor. The platform has enabled me to reach more people, explore complex topics, and build a business that works for my life. I'm especially grateful to Kathe Sweeney, who took a chance on me as an instructor, signing me (with then Lynda.com) when I was 24.

Even more personally, I have so much gratitude for my friends, Erika, Nadia, and BEFNS. For a decade+ you've had my back, sitting with me in every struggle and celebrating with me in every win.

My dad, whose lighthearted humor, eye for detail, and steadfast support have been a bedrock for my life endeavors.

My sister, who's been my best friend since I was 5 and makes me belly laugh in a way no one else does.

My husband, who has unconditionally loved me through so many seasons of life. You inspire me to live authentically, be curious, and not take life so seriously. And you gave me what I'm most grateful for of all, our son. I love you.

About the Author

Elizabeth Lotardo is a consultant, writer, and online instructor who helps organizations drive emotional engagement.

Elizabeth writes for *Harvard Business Review* and is the co-author of *Selling with Noble Purpose*. Her work has been featured in *The Wall Street Journal* and on NPR.

With an undergraduate degree in advertising from Boston University and a Master's in Industrial and Organizational Psychology, Elizabeth works with senior leaders, frontline managers, and entry-level teammates to create more purpose-driven work experiences. Her clients include Salesforce, DraftKings, Hilton, and numerous Berkshire Hathaway organizations.

She is also a popular LinkedIn Learning instructor who designs workshops on topics like Leading without Formal Authority, Finding Your Purpose at Work, and Leading Yourself.

Index

228

Index

229

230

232

Index